D1478987

DESIGN OF
CHILDREN'S PLAY
ENVIRONMENTS

DESIGN OF CHILDREN'S PLAY ENVIRONMENTS

Mitsuru Senda

Architect, Dr. Eng.
Professor, Nagoya Institute of Technology
Nagoya, Japan

McGraw-Hill, Inc.
New York St. Louis San Francisco Auckland Bogotá
Caracas Lisbon London Madrid Mexico Milan
Montreal New Delhi Paris San Juan Singapore
Sydney Tokyo Toronto

Library of Congress Cataloging-in-Publication Data

Senda, Mitsuru.
  Design of children's play environments / Mitsuru Senda.
    p.   cm.
  Includes index.
  ISBN 0-07-056213-X
  1. Playgrounds—Planning. 2. Playgrounds—Design and
  construction. 3. Recreation areas—Planning. 4. Recreation
  areas—Design and construction. I. Title.
  GV425.S45 1992   91-34725
  711'.558—dc20   CIP

2 3 4 5 6 7 8 9 0   DOR/DOR   9 8 7 6 5 4 3 2

ISBN 0-07-056213-X

*The sponsoring editor for this book was Joel E. Stein, the
editing supervisor was Caroline Levine, the designer was
Susan Maksuta, and the production supervisor was Donald F.
Schmidt. It was set in Times Roman on a Macintosh system*

*Printed and bound by Impresora Donneco Internacional
S.A. de C.V., a division of R. R. Donnelley & Sons Company.*

Manufactured in Mexico

CONTENTS

3 Theory and Design of "Parks" and Architecture for Children..........97

PREFACE

Children are frequently the most oppressed group of people in the world today. Children are persecuted by adults not only in developing countries but also in developed ones. The form this oppression takes may differ between developing and developed countries but the one point that remains in both is that adults have taken away from children a way of life that is intrinsic to them.

Children, who have the natural right to experience healthy and happy childhoods, are being oppressed in many ways. Children do not have the vote. They do not have the right to say "no" or the right to choose.

Adults often unwittingly persecute children also in areas and equipment they provide for play. Adults have praised children by saying that they are geniuses who can invent play anywhere at any time and on this excuse have destroyed spaces set aside for play and included it in their own space. This tendency has been particularly strong in Japan during the past forty years. No recognition was given to the importance and significance of the living and playing space for children and there was no scientific foundation for securing this space. Adults were depriving children of space and equipment for play at will.

I have been studying the environment and the mechanism of children's play in Japan and have been designing structures and spaces based on these studies. I believe that the fruits of these studies on children in Japan and designs developed from them are not peculiar to Japan and will provide a solution to the problems which are common to children throughout this computerized and internationalized world of today.

Twenty-odd years ago, after graduating from the university, I was working at the outdoor school at the Central Children's Land in Yokohama as a member of the staff for Kiyonori Kikutake. At that time, the well-known sculptor, Isamu Noguchi, was supervising the design of a Children's Play Park at the Central Children's Land along with Yukio Otani, a prominent architect. Since I was working on the same site, I often had the opportunity of seeing Mr. Noguchi at work. I once saw him supervising the construction of a round earth mound and ordering the bulldozer operator to take a further 5 cm off. This was the incident which drew my attention away from simple architectural design to the larger-scale design that took in the surrounding ground.

When I later went independent and founded the Environment Design Institute, the first commission I received was for the design of a play structure. It was around the time I designed the model playground at the Central Children's Hall in Sendai that I decided to make the design of children's play environments the central theme of my work. The special feature "Let's Make Trees for the City" in the magazine "Toshi Jutaku" (Urban Housing) was in a way my manifesto concerning the design of children's play environments.

Once, I was invited to give a talk to the Society for Studies on Children and showed them the slides of my work for the design of such play environments. An elderly academic there said to me, "Children will discover and invent play in any kind of place. What is the point of your design?" This was quite a blow to me. I had simply been designing play structures because it was fun. It was then that I began to make a study on "children's play environments" in parallel with my design work.

I began to think about the significance of design of play environments and was able to conduct research on this subject with funding I obtained as the first recipient of the Toyota Foundation's research grant in 1974. I published the results of my research under the title of "Children's Play Environment—Why Do We Study and Design Children's Playgrounds?" in the magazine "Kenchiku-Bunka" (Architecture and Culture) in 1977.

In 1982, I put together the results of my study in a thesis, which I submitted to my alma mater. This paper was later rewritten for the general public. Published under the title "Children's Play Environments" from Chikuma Shobo in 1984, it received an award from the International Association of Traffic and Safety Sciences. I was awarded a research grant by the National Institute for Research Advancement (NIRA) in 1985 and 1986 for "Study on the Preparation of the Master Plan for Children's Play Environments."

The circumstances surrounding children have changed greatly over the past thirty years, and the speed of the change appears to be accelerating. I believe, however, that the play environment children require has remained and will remain the same in essence. The design of the play environment is not simply the design of playgrounds. Buildings, streets, parks, and rivers are all playgrounds for children. We adults have classified them, however, according to their functions as architectural structures, urban areas, roads, parkland, and utilities and have entrusted their design to different people such as architects, landscape designers, urban planners, and industrial designers. This is one of the factors impoverishing the living environments for children.

To design a play environment for children is to design cities, buildings, parks, roads, and utilities from the point of view of children. My work is to design buildings, parks, play structures, and displays for children. This book, therefore, deals not simply with the design of children's playgrounds but with all areas affecting a child's life.

In the first and second chapters of this book, I explain the theory behind my work and what is involved in the design of play structures and playgrounds, giving actual examples. In Chapter 3, I deal with what I call "parks" and architecture for children using photographs and illustrations.

A number of my works have been published in journals outside of Japan. These include the five play structures and buildings described on pages 114 to 127 of "Spielraum für Kinder," a German publication. The giant play structure in Sendai was also taken up by "Spielraum für Kinder" and then in the Italiian design magazine *Abitare,* and seems to have exerted a significant influence on major play structures, such as the "Dragon" at the Parc de la Villette in France.

The House of Nature for Young People in Okinawa and the Children's Center in Kagoshima were published in "Baumeister" and "L'Architecture d'Aujourd'hui." The Banana House was shown at the Architectural Biennale held at the Pompidou Center in Paris in 1984, while my circular play system theory received an airing in "Garten und Landschaft," a German landscapers' magazine, in 1989. As has already been mentioned, the design of the play environment for children set forth in this book is applicable to children throughout the world.

I hope this book will contribute in its own small way to the creation of better play environments for children everywhere.

Mitsuru Senda

Credits

COVER DESIGN: Shin Matsunaga

Photographs: Fujitsuka Mitsumasa

Yoshio Shiratori

Tomio Ohashi

Yutaka Suzuki

Katsuaki Furudate

Koji Murakoshi

The Japan Architect

Shinkenchiku-sha Co., Ltd.

Shoukokusha Publishing Co.,Ltd.

Kotobuki Corporation

Structure of the Play Environment

WHAT DOES PLAY MEAN TO CHILDREN?

For a child, play must be the whole of his or her life, or at least, it must be at the center of his or her life. Children learn, make friends, and nurture their creativity through play.

For a child, playing must be his or her business. Like Mark Twain's Tom Sawyer and Huckleberry Finn, the child must think seriously about how to play and how to make play fun.

If there is a log by the road, a child will jump onto it and walk along it balancing him or herself. Another child jumps onto the log at the other end, and the two meet in the middle and start pushing each other. Scenes like this are found everywhere. There is first the act of a child jumping onto the log, which is an act of leaping away from the ordinary and routine, and then a game of pushing starts and the child makes a friend. This is what play is for children, jumping away from the ordinary.

The Japanese word for play, "asobi," has three meanings, just as in English the word "play" can be used with reference also to musical or theatrical performances. One of the meanings of the word "asobi" in Japanese is its original meaning of play as opposed to "work." Another is to depart from the ordinary, to break out from the set form. It is in this sense that we refer to creative art as "asobi." A third meaning is that of spare room and allowance. Cogwheels, for example, require gaps between them to function properly. This gap, the allowance required to ensure smooth and efficient functioning of the wheels, is called "asobi." When we talk of children's play, we, of course, normally use the word in the first sense given above, but the word "asobi" in Japanese can also refer to the effect of allowing things to function smoothly. I tend to think of children's play in the second sense of "asobi" given above. Play in my view is the departure from the routine and the ordinary. Of course, children's play is nothing extraordinary, but only a child can walk along a log, which is nothing out of the ordinary for the adult, as if he or she were doing something extraordinary like crossing a narrow bridge across a deep valley.

"Children are geniuses at play. They will invent play in any place at any time and will turn any place into a playground. To give them play structures and playgrounds is to pluck their inventiveness for play in the bud. There is no need to provide them with play structures and playgrounds." This is the kind of opinion which has been thrown at me time and time again. Everyone in the world was once a child him or herself and therefore has the qualifications to be an expert on children's play and playgrounds. Unfortunately, however, no one can ever have the experience of another's childhood. True, we did not have playgrounds specially set aside for us when we were children, but this does not mean that the circumstances surrounding children today are such that they do not need to be provided with playgrounds and play structures.

I am convinced that the theory that children are geniuses is what has deprived children of their play and playgrounds in cities. "Children do not need playgrounds. They will turn any place into a playground."

This is the line of thought which has allowed woods and open spaces to be converted into buildings in the course of urban development and has provided the excuse for taking away children's playgrounds. We see today that as a result children have lost their handholds on play, like ants which have fallen into a glass. This is the reality of the play environment for children in a modern city. Children have lost the opportunities to show their true genius. I too believe that "children are geniuses." That is why I would like to exclaim in a loud voice the precondition that "children must be given an environment in which they can display their genius." We must secure, plan, and design environments in cities where children can display this genius.

FEW ADULTS HAVE INTEREST IN CHILDREN'S PLAYGROUNDS!

Every adult has some opinion on children's play and playgrounds. This is simply because every adult was once him or herself a child. Surprisingly few adults, on the other hand, actually take any positive interest in children's playgrounds or do anything about improving them.

According to a survey I conducted in a city in Japan with a population of around 300,000, only 30 percent of the grown-ups were interested in children's play. Basically, it is only parents with children of preschool or primary school age who show any interest in children's play environments. Once the child has reached the top grades of primary school or entered junior high school the parents begin to consider their study to be far more important and lose interest in their children's play. Many will go so far as to oppose construction of playgrounds and preschools in the vicinity of their homes because of the noise the children will make.

In most cases, it is found that the children of these people have at least reached junior high school age. People who continue to have an interest in environments for children are almost nonexistent.

INSISTENCE ON SAFETY INHIBITS CHILDREN AT PLAY

There are people who work for children. There are grown-ups who gather groups of children in parks and play with them. But what happens if there is an accident? The grown-up will be held responsible in Japan regardless of whether he or she is being paid to look after the children. Preschools and schools are also liable to prosecution. This situation often makes people who are willing to help children hesitate, while the case in which an adult, on seeing children engaged in dangerous play, will simply pass by ignoring them is the other side of the same coin.

This excessive emphasis on safety pervades preschools, schools, and parks. Children can die in a pool of water less than 10 cm in depth. A child may die if he or she falls the wrong way from a height of 1 m. But then, what will happen if all streams or pools of water are fenced off and made inaccessible? Children will be deprived of the chance to play in water and the chance to try their daring by jumping from a height. The corollary is that their healthy growth will be impeded.

Preschools, schools, and parks are all pervaded by this insistence on safety, and utmost care is taken to ensure that the children are not exposed to the slightest danger, but children must learn how to avoid great dangers by being exposed to small dangers. The fact that children are not allowed to experience small dangers means that they will be totally unprepared when they are exposed to greater ones.

Play structures are gradually being removed from preschools and schools which have fallen under this spell of overemphasis on safety. The system of safety insurance is another factor contributing to this. Preschools and school where there are play structures and ponds have to pay higher insurance premiums. The result is that children are enclosed in a cage called safety.

Grown-ups must think again about what children need during their period of growth. Grown-ups must provide children with environments that will give them opportunities to learn about small dangers and how to avoid them.

CHILDREN ARE THE BUILDERS OF OUR FUTURE

Desmond Morris, the British zoologist, has said that play has creativity as its bonus. In various ways the play environment for children throughout the world is being exposed to the risk of extinction today. Children in Asian countries, such as Japan, China, Korea, and Taiwan, are losing their playgrounds to urban development and their play time to high-level competition in school exams. TV and TV games have transformed the mode of children's play to that in which they play alone in their rooms. Children in the United States and Europe are perhaps a little more fortunate. Children in Munich, for example, are endowed with four times (twenty times if we consider only the parkland) as much playing space as that in Tokyo.

In general, however, the worldwide trend is toward restricting children from playing outdoors because of the fear for their safety and the real dangers of kidnapping, as well as because of the proliferation of indoor activities, notably TV viewing and TV games. The corollary will be the lowering of the creativity of children, who must be the builders of the future. Provision of an environment that will nurture children's creativity is a task we adults must tackle with the same energy and urgency that we apply to such problems as the global environment.

IMPORTANCE OF RESEARCH AND DESIGN FOR PLAY

There has in the past been no adequate scientific research on children's need for space for play and no data had been given on what kind of mechanisms were required in the spaces and equipment for play, with the result that adults were gradually encroaching upon children's space.

Adults paid no attention to children's play, saying "Children are geniuses at play and will invent play by themselves." Today we are beginning to pay for our negligence in the past. Children are beginning to suffocate in urban environments. An increasing number of children are suffering from stress, and there has been a marked rise in the cases of children suffering from adult diseases and autism, of children refusing to attend school, of violence and bullying in schools, and of children committing suicide.

One of the major causes of these various symptoms children are suffering, I believe, is the deterioration of the play environment. Research on children's play was in the past conducted separately from the points of view of pedagogy, pediatry, pedology, and child psychology and of architecture, housing science, landscaping, and urban planning. In other words, there was no research from an overall point of view. I am an architect by training but have for the past 25 years been conducting a comprehensive study on the subject of play environments for children, and the fruits of my research have been reflected in my designs for play environments. Since this is not an academic publication, I am merely giving here the results of the research, but clearly research on children's play and design based on this research are gaining in importance.

FOUR ELEMENTS OF PLAY ENVIRONMENTS

A child's play environment consists of four elements, a place to play, time to play, friends to play with, and what they actually do. All four elements are indispensable and, at the same time, are mutually interrelated in a complex web. A rich play environment requires sufficient time and space in which to play. Four to five hours per day, for example, of outdoor play and 1 to 2 ha of space near home would be suitable for a twelve-year-old child. There should always be from four or five up to ten playmates, and the manner in which they play should desirably range from traditional games such as hopscotch, ball games, and leapfrog to the more modern sporty games. A child's play time in Japan has dropped nearly 40 percent over the past forty years, while the average play space today of about 3000 square meters is a tenth to a twentieth of what it once was. The number of friends with whom a child plays has also been dramatically reduced. A child today normally plays with two or three other children of the same age. The number of games children play in Japan was reduced to somewhere between a half and a third of what it was over the twenty-year period between 1955 and 1975. TV games have further reduced this number.

The play environment has seen dramatic changes in Japan. The rapid industrial growth of Japan once made her notorious for pollution. Perhaps she is today leading the way in the world in the dramatic deterioration of children's play environments.

ROLES OF EQUIPMENT AND SPACE

Equipment for children's play, which I call play structures, must provide the starting point for children's play activities. They must be catalysts in generating play. The same can be said of the space in which they play. This too must be such that it will spontaneously entice children into playing. A good play space will lead children to play freely and without restriction.

I outline below the basic elements required for the equipment and spaces that will entice children to play and then move on to give examples of my design for such equipment and spaces.

STRUCTURE OF SPACE AND EQUIPMENT FOR PLAY

My research suggests that satisfactory play space and equipment have the following seven requirements.

1. There must be a circulation of play. That is to say, there must be a clear flow of movement which comprises one big activity.

2. The process must be safe but rich in variety.

3. The process must not be singularly patterned and must have shortcuts and bypasses.

4. The process must entail symbolic high places.

5. The process must contain parts where children can experience "dizziness."

6. The process must offer large and small gathering places.

7. The process as a whole must not be closed. It must be open and have a number of access routes.

I have termed spaces and equipment which satisfy these seven conditions "circular play systems."

These are the conclusions reached through various studies I conducted over a period of ten years or so between 1973 and 1982. The fundamental principles were deduced from considerations given to the structures of spaces that generate group play among children in the following three studies.

1. Study on the initiation of play on play structures.

2. Study on the initiation of play in playgrounds.

3. Study on the initiation of play on residential areas.

I shall discuss this theory and its application in the following chapters.

Theory and Design of Play Structures and Playgrounds

2

ROLE OF PLAY STRUCTURES

Everyone recognizes the necessity of play for children, but many adults do not recognize the need of play structures, claiming that children will discover and create their own games, together with the structures and places necessary for them. The reality, however, is that in Japan children's playgrounds have almost been annihilated except where they are preserved in the form of children's parks. Children used to have open spaces, woods, hills, and streams around them, but these have been lost and replaced today by housing and office buildings. The theory that "children are geniuses at play and there is no need therefore to go out of the way to provide them with places and things to play with" has turned the empty spaces and unused land which were the spaces where children played into functional buildings. Children in Japan today have very little space they can freely play in. They need to have equipment and spaces set aside that will entice them to play provided for them in the form of play structures and playgrounds.

Play structures, however, cannot provide for all of the children's playing requirements. They will cater perhaps to 25 percent of children's playing needs but cannot make up for playing in natural environments, such as play using grass and flowers and ball games in open spaces.

Play structures can provide for about a quarter of children's play activities in a concentrated way. An important role of play structures is to concentrate children's play into small areas.

DEVELOPMENT STAGES OF PLAY ON PLAY STRUCTURES

There are stages in the development of play on play structures. Take, for example, the playground slide. When a small child first uses a slide, the child will stand at the top of the slide, look around, and then sit down and slide down. After repeating this procedure several times, the child will start sliding down not just sitting but lying down, pushing him or herself with his or her hands or traveling head first. Then, if a friend appears on the scene, they will try sliding down together, or one of them will climb up the slide and pull the other's feet or start playing tag around the slide. We notice here that there are three stages to the mode of play. The first stage might be termed the "stage of functional play." This is the stage of play at which the child first experiences the function of play that is proper to the play structure. On a slide this is the stage of sliding sitting down. After repeating this stage several times, the child moves on to the "stage of technical play." Instead of just sliding in the sitting position, the child starts inventing new ways of using the slide, such as pushing him or herself with his or her hands, sliding down head first or lying down. On a swing this is the stage at which the child stands up on the swing. It is the stage in which the child has fun while improving his or her techniques. Once the child has passed this stage, he or she moves on to the "stage of social play" and starts playing games using the play structures as a medium. When they start playing tag on a slide, the proper function of the slide as a slide becomes less important. The slide, the play structure, becomes simply a stage setting for the game and the children concentrate on playing tag.

Children change the way in which they play on play structures in this way, but not all play activities on such structures go through these three stages of "functional," "technical," and "social" play.

Some play structures lend themselves easily only to the "stage of functional play" and will not prompt the development of the activities into the stages of "technical" and "social" play.

Swings, for example, lend themselves to the "stage of technical play," but it is difficult for the activities on swings to develop into games, which is the "stage of social play." Swings, in other words, are structures made for individual play. Jungle gyms, on the other hand, are simple devices but easily lead to the stage of "technical" play. At the same time, the stage of technical play is liable to generate competition, and competition thus generated can be regarded as social, depending on what the techniques involve.

It can be seen from these observations that development of play on structures that easily lend themselves to the three stages of "functional," "technical," and "social" play agrees with the development of children's play itself. (See Fig. 2.1.) Children will first acquire the basic skills, improve on them, and use them to play games.

INITIATION OF GAMES ON PLAY STRUCTURES

What sort of play structures, then, lend themselves to this development of play in stages up to that of "social" play? Observations were made on the way in which games are created by children playing on play structures. The play structures used were

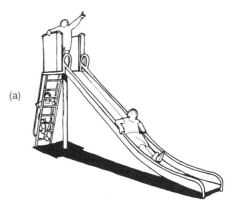
(a)

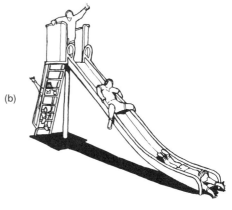
(b)

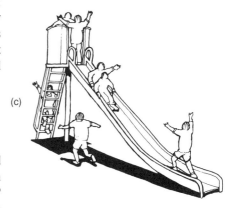
(c)

Fig. 2.1 Development stages of play on play structures: (a) "functional" play, (b)"technical" play, (c) "social" play.

Fig. 2.2 Initiation of games on play structures. From left top to below. Abacus Slider, Circulation, Jungle Gym, Climbing Arrangement Poly Play, Crow's Nest, Ropeway, Play Sculpture, Suspension Bridge, Small Land, Cosmos, Time Tunnel, Pokot.

five types each of traditional play structures in children's playgrounds, wooden play structures imported from Europe, and new play structures designed by my firm and university. (See Fig. 2.2.)

The games generated on these play structures can be divided into (1) competition games, (2) chase games, (3) fighting games, and (4) imitation games.

An example of competition games is that in which children race down a double slide.

Chase games are games such as tag and "cops and robbers" in which children chase and catch each other. In a way these are the most basic forms of games.

Fighting games are games like wrestling and sword fighting.

Imitation games are those in which children pretend to be shopping, at school, or housekeeping, using the play structures as backgrounds.

A characteristic of play structures used for competition games is that they allow for variety in the flow of play. The "Abacus Slider," for example, can be used by several children sliding down at the same time, and the children can compare the speed and the ways in which they slide.

Play structures used for chase games have clearly defined flow patterns. These flow patterns contain elements of "dizziness," such as sliding and jumping. In "Circulation," for example, the flow patterns themselves are made into a play structure and entail actions like "sliding," "climbing," "jumping down," and "running." It also contains a large number of dead angles providing variation and surprise and is extremely well designed for chase games.

Fighting games usually take place on play structures which have soft floors, nets, urethane mats, suspension bridges, and sand pits and which form some kind of an enclosure.

Imitation games can be divided into those such as playing at being trains and airplanes, which involve "dizziness" actions of "sliding" and "jumping," and those like playing at housekeeping, which are not directly related to the functions of the play structures. The first of these are more common on play structures, and the latter are rarely observed.

The element of challenge has an important role in play structures like "Jungle Gyms," "Climbing Arrangement Poly Play," and "Crow's Nest." Once the children have overcome the challenges the structure loses its attraction and the activities tend not to develop into other games. When there is a leader figure or some keen proposer of the game, they can be used for certain kinds of games but under normal conditions do not lead to such games.

"Swings," "Seesaws," "Ropeways," and "Abacus Sliders" are all play structures which lead from the "stage of functional play" to the "stage of technical play." They have large elements of "dizziness," which make up nearly 70 percent of the activities on them. Since the experience of "dizziness" is something that is not a part of ordinary life, these provide attractive play opportunities for children. These play structures, however, generate a lot of repetition and will lead in continuous stages to "technical play" but not to "social play."

Since the activities on these play structures are generally simple, they tend to be used by children in preschool or the lower grades of primary school.

Play structures which lend themselves to "social play" and easily generate games include "Slides," "Play Sculpture," "Suspension Bridge," "Small Land," "Cosmos," and "Circulation." A characteristic of these structures is that they allow for the development of play in the stages of "functional," "technical," and "social" play. In terms of the amount of time spent, the elements of "rest" and "challenge" take up about 40 percent each of the play activities on these structures, while "dizziness" makes up the remaining 20 percent. Although the actions involved in the element of "dizziness" have a relatively small proportion in terms of duration, since they are mostly instantaneous actions such as jumping, sliding, and swinging, they would occupy the same proportion as "rest" and "challenge" in terms of frequency. These play structures, in other words, are all-round multifunction structures.

The "dizziness" function occupies an important place among the factors generating games on these play structures. On the "Suspension Bridge," for example, it is difficult for children to swing the bridge by themselves. The bridge will swing only when a few children cooperate. While swinging the bridge, the children experience the thrill that the bridge might fall. Small children will have to hold tight onto the sides. Once someone becomes frightened, others will shout at each other to swing the bridge even more. In this way, the "dizziness" function of "swinging" generates a game among the children and makes the game fun. "Small Land" too contains a "dizziness" mechanism in its small suspension bridges and stainless slides.

"Time Tunnel" has two small slides inside, and these dark slides seem to increase the fun for children on this structure. "Cosmos" has a kind of slide in the hollow at the top of it. There is a hole at the end of the slide which a child can go into up to his or her head, and the children can enjoy the sensation of falling down.

"Pokot" and "Circulation" are structures on different scales but are composite play structures with a similar content. "Circulation" is a structure which covers all kinds of actions from climbing, sliding, and jumping down to going underground. The reason this structure stimulated the generation of games, provided so much fun for the children, and was popular with them was that it had a urethane mat floor. Among the sensations of "dizziness," jumping through the air is more thrilling than sliding. Because there was a thick mattress (250 mm) on the floor, children could jump from great heights without any fear. This jumping action, or act of "throwing oneself off," was made a part of the game, and fighting and wrestling also occurred on this structure. Play is made much more fun and dynamic for children by these actions for experiencing "dizziness," which I would term the "action of throwing oneself off."

The difference between the 2 m by 2 m "Pokot" and the 5 m by 5 m "Circulation" seems to lie not so much in whether you could wrestle on the urethane mat but in the speed of play on them. "Circulation" is popular with children up to the upper grades of primary school, and the reason for this is thought to lie in the capacity of the structure to allow speedy actions.

One of the characteristics of play structures which generate games is their function of circulation. We have mentioned above the games played on such play structures, and they are basically variations of "tag." Some of the children run away while others chase them. In such games the continuity of the actions becomes an important element. Slides, for example, provide circular flow patterns in their simplest form, while on structures like "Suspension Bridge," "Small Land," and "Time Tunnel," the tunnels and bridges make up the flow patterns. The popular "Circulation," too, is designed in such a way that children can run around the outside of the 5-m-square structure. On structures like "Pokot" and "Cosmos," which do not have clear flow patterns, the holes which give the structures a porous form and mazelike flow patterns have an important role in generating games.

Looking at the play structures from the point of view of changes in the actions and experiences of the children, there is a feature common to all structures which easily leads to the generation of games. Such structures have contrasting component elements. "Circulation," for example, has contrasting spaces of a dark, narrow tunnel and a high, open bridge. Most of the children jump up and down when they come out of the pitch-dark tunnel into the bright deck, and it seems as if they are at their most energetic and ready for more adventure.

On "Cosmos," secretive play is observed in the encapsulated cozy space inside the canvas, while open games such as tag are the main games played on the steel pipes on the outside. It is the existence of these two contrasting elements which seems to be making play on this structure fun.

There is little else to do on the "Time Tunnel" except go through the tunnel itself but one section in the tunnel is difficult for children to climb. This combination of easy and difficult is another means of developing the way in which children play.

CIRCULAR PLAY SYSTEMS

An understanding of the makeup of play structures which easily lead to the initiation of games can be gained through a study of games played on play structures. Their characteristics may be summarized as follows.

1. There must be an overall circulation of play.

2. Children must be able to experience variation within the circle.

3. The circle must contain a symbolic high point.

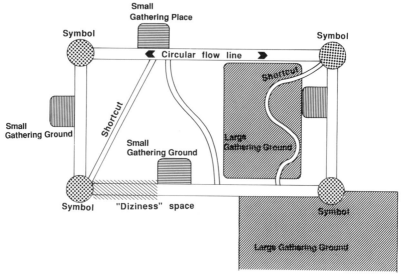

Fig. 2.3 Model of a circular play system.

4. The circle must contain a place where children can experience "dizziness."

5. The circle must contain large and small gathering places.

6. There must be shortcuts.

7. The circle must be accessible through a number of points so that it comprises a "porous" space.

See Fig. 2.3.

DEVELOPMENT OF THE DESIGN OF PLAY STRUCTURES

Giant Play Structures

This was my first design concept for a play structure, which I made in 1968. The idea behind it was that play structures must be in the nature of large trees.

A large tree is a complex of play functions on which you can hang a rope and play

Tarzan, which you can climb, and on which you can build secret tree houses. I thought that a multifunction, composite play structure would help generate richer play activities than a single-function play structure. I believed that the ambiguity of the functions contained in such a structure would give children the opportunity to freely invent new games.

Children's play not only consists of active elements like rolling and jumping but also involves resting and lazing about. Play environment equipment too is composed of these contrasting elements. Children like bright places but they like even more dark and secretive places. Play takes in contrasting elements of wide open spaces and narrow, constricted spaces, high and low places, as well as soft and hard places. Children simultaneously hold the desire to fly through the air and the desire to go down into a hole. A giant play structure is one which combines the contrasting spatial elements.

Giant Path Play Structure—Sendai

This was the first giant play structure I designed in 1968. It is a pipe coil 1 m in diameter and 180 m in length and is made up of four different kinds of 8-m units. Peculiar to this structure among the four types of units is the trifurcate unit, which can be joined to give a hexagonal layout. (See Figs. 2.4 to 2.11.) This structure was taken up by "Spielraum für Kinder," a German publication on playgrounds, in 1976, and by the Italian design magazine *Abitare*, and seems to have exerted significant influence on major play structures, such as the "Dragon" at Parc de la Villette in France. Different materials were used in its construction, but the composite functions of the "Dragon" are substantially reproduced from mine.(See Figs. 2.12 and 2.13.)

Fig. 2.4 Giant Path play structure. Children's play structures must also be aesthetically pleasing. (*Photo: Yoshio Shiratori.*)

Fig. 2.5 Giant Path play structure. Units 1.8 m long and 1 m in diameter are joined together. (*Photo: Yoshio Shiratori.*)

Fig. 2.6 Giant Path play structure. The long slide leads to a large hollow from the triangular jungle gym. (*Photo: Yoshio Shiratori.*)

Fig. 2.7 Giant Path play structure. (*Photo: Yoshio Shiratori.*)

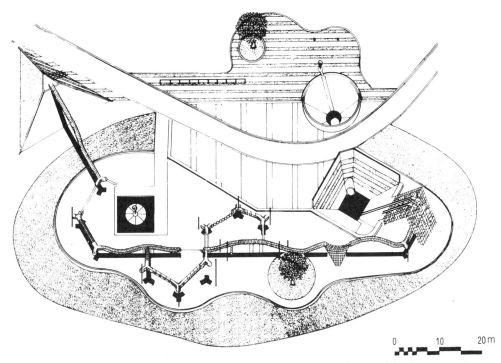

Fig. 2.8 Layout of Giant Path play structure. Various shapes are created by combining four types of units.

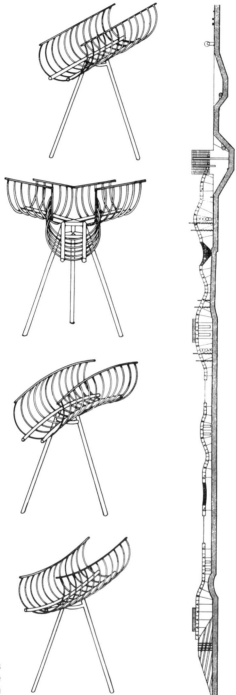

Fig. 2.9 The four types of units used in the Giant Path play structure.

Fig. 2.10 Giant Path play structure. Variation in the vision height.

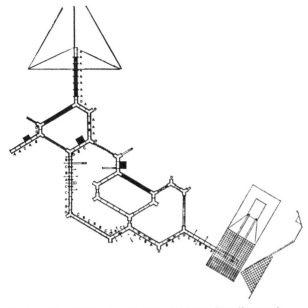

Fig. 2.11 Giant Path play structure. Horizontally self-repeating patterns are created by combining the units.

Fig. 2.12 The Dragon, Parc de la Villette, Paris.

Fig. 2.13 The Dragon, Parc de la Villette, Paris.

The Dragon

This is a play structure in the Children's Land in Aichi Prefecture. Various devices are built into a tube 2 m in diameter and 200 m in length to create an environment for play. (See Figs. 2.14 to 2.16.)

Giant Tube Play Structure

The "Fun Tube" in the Children's Plaza at the Science Expo in Tsukuba in 1985 was a development of the two structures mentioned above. The tube is 2.7 m in diameter and 270 m long. The height of the tube varies from 45 cm to 3.5 m above the ground and the tube comprises a path rich in variety with an ascent, viewpoint, and descent.

The tube contains seven scientific-experience devices. In the "Wind Tunnel," children can experience a wind speed of 20 m, while in the "Scope Tunnel," they can experience a widening of the field of vision using fish-eye, wide-angle, and pinhole lenses. The "Mist Tunnel," as its name suggests, produces mist, and in the "Echo Tunnel" children can hear their voices coming back to them with a strange resonance. (See Figs. 2.17 to 2.24.)

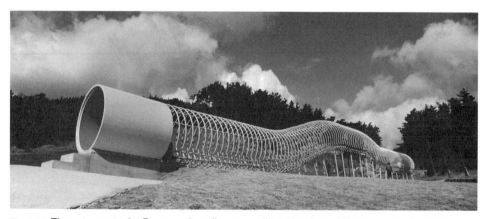

Fig. 2.14 The entrance to the Dragon—2-m-diameter coils, 200 m long. (*Photo: Yoshio Shiratori.*)

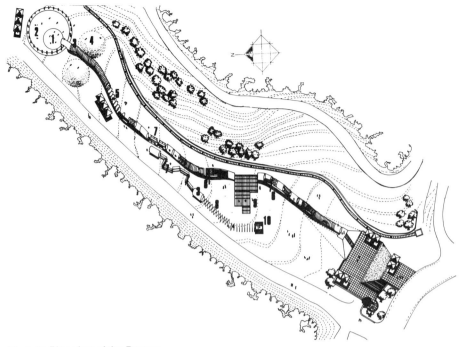

Fig. 2.15 Plan view of the Dragon.

Giant Footbridge Play Structure

This design was published in 1970. Instead of making footbridges simply a means of

Fig. 2.16 Dragon. (*Photo: Yoshio Shiratori.*)

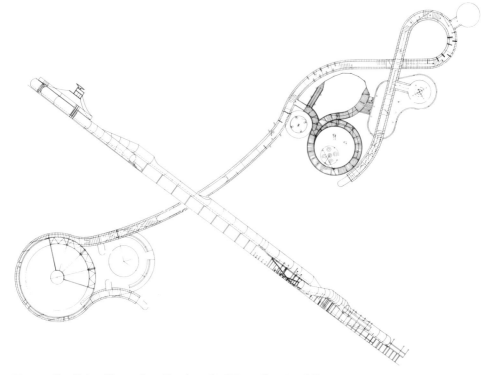

Fig. 2.17 Fun Tube. Plan and section. Length: 270 m, diameter: 2.7 m.

Fig. 2.18 Inside of the Fun Tube. (*Photo: Fujitsuka Mitsumasa.*)

Fig. 2.19 Inside of the Fun Tube. (*Photo: Fujitsuka Mitsumasa.*)

Fig. 2.20 Inside of the Fun Tube. (*Photo: Fujitsuka Mitsumasa.*)

Fig. 2.21 Inside of the Fun Tube. (*Photo: Fujitsuka Mitsumasa.*)

Fig. 2.22 Inside of the Fun Tube. (*Photo: Fujitsuka Mitsumasa.*)

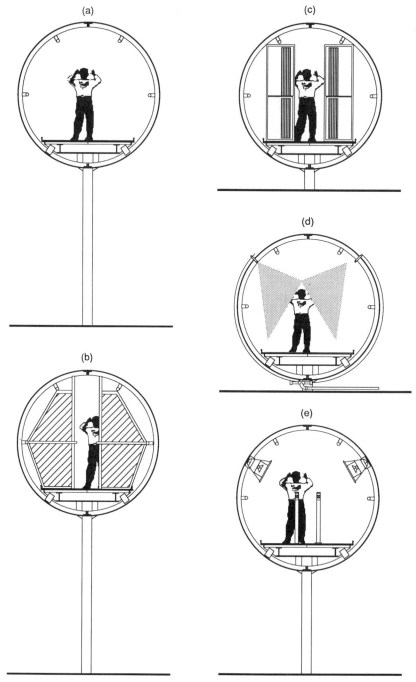

Fig. 2.23 Variation inside the Fun Tube: (a) Typical section, (b) Mirror Tunnel, (c) Wind Tunnel, (d) Fog Tunnel, (e) Echo Tunnel, (f) Scope Tunnel, (g) Silent Tunnel, (h) Water Tunnel.

(f)

(g)

(h)

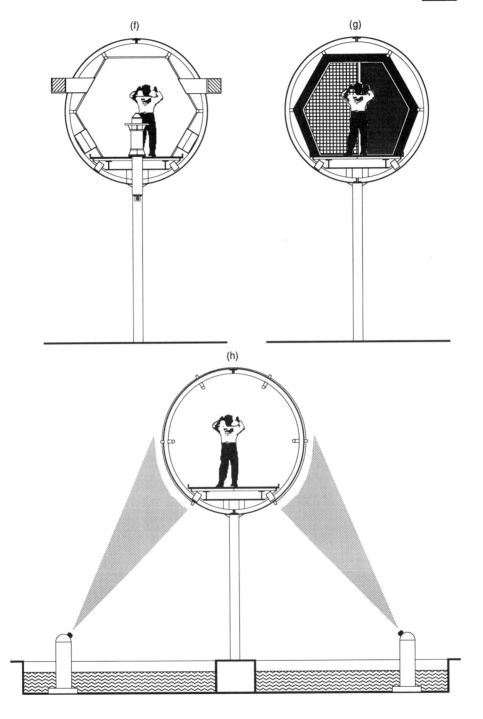

Fig. 2.24 Fun Tube. (*Photo: Fujitsuka Mitsumasa.*)

crossing roads, they were designed so that crossing them in itself is a playful experience for children. (See Fig. 2.25.)

Giant Tower Play Structure

Instead of simply having the children go up and down the steps in a vertical line, the tower was designed so that children would climb up and down the play structure and use the ground floor, the roof, and the floors in between (Figs. 2.26, 2.27, and 2.28). The structure shown in Fig. 2.27 was named the "Children's Elevator."

Giant Stairway Play Structure

The wooden play structure in Fig. 2.29 was designed in the form of a stairway on a slope 90 m long and with a height difference of 15 m. Figure 2.30 is an axonometric projection of a giant stairway play structure.

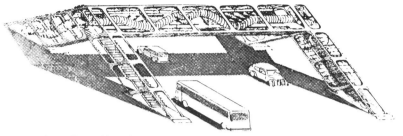

Fig. 2.25 Giant Footbridge play structure.

Fig. 2.26 Giant Tower play structure. The Giant Tower play structure at the Akita Prefectural Children's Center. (*Photo: Katsuaki Furudate.*)

Fig. 2.27 Giant Tower play structure. The Children's Elevator at Hamamatsu Science Museum. The stairway climbs up around the Giant Tower play structure. The whole structure is made up of a steel wire net, and parents can watch their children going up and down on the inside. (*Photo: Fujitsuka Mitsumasa.*)

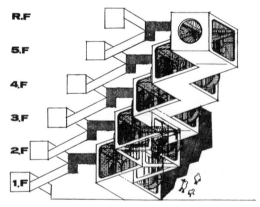

Fig. 2.28 Giant Tower play structure attached to apartment block stairways.

Fig. 2.29 Giant Wooden Stairway play structure, 90 m in length and with a height difference of 15 m. (*Photo: Shoukokusha Publishing Co., Ltd.*)

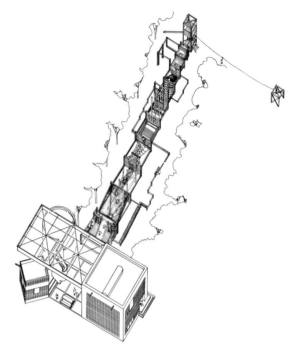

Fig. 2.30 Akita Prefectural Children's Center and Giant Stairway play structure. Axonometric projection.

Giant Tent Play Structure

This is a giant play structure in the form of a tent 23 m in diameter (Figs. 2.31 and 2.32). A spiral staircase in the center leads up to the 6-m-high viewpoint. The outside of the tent becomes a 9-m slide (Fig. 2.33). The floor inside the tent is given a rubber chip finish to provide an area where children can play freely in the shade.

Giant Slope Play Structure 1

This is a giant play structure set on the slope of a hill (Figs. 2.34 and 2.35).

Giant Slope Play Structure 2

This is a giant play structure with slopes as its main theme. (See Figs. 2.36 to 2.40.)

Slopes can provide unstable and stimulating spots for children. Slope equipment which by nature contains a "dizziness" experience is effective in generating active play by breaking down the ordinary feeling of the site.

Giant Earth Play Structure

The undulating land itself was turned into a giant play structure. This structure, designed in 1970, consists of "waves" of earth 2.5 m

Fig. 2.31 Giant Tent play structure. The space underneath the tent is a large playground in the shade. (*Photo: Fujitsuka Mitsumasa.*)

Fig. 2.32 Giant Tent play structure. (*Photo: Fujitsuka Mitsumasa.*)

high and 30 m long set at 12-m intervals, together with several 90-m-long white logs mounted on top of them. (See Figs. 2.41 and 2.42.)

Circular Play Structures

The linear giant play structures are not very good for generating circulation play. Once the structure has been "conquered," there is no repetition and they do not easily lead to games like tag and chase. Their strong points, in other words, are for actions of moving from A to B and of "conquest" but not for games.

I began a study on the behavior of children during play on play structures in 1979 and in 1982 published a paper on the makeup of play structures which easily lead to games and which I termed the "circular play system."

I named play structures which had a circular theme "circular play structures." To

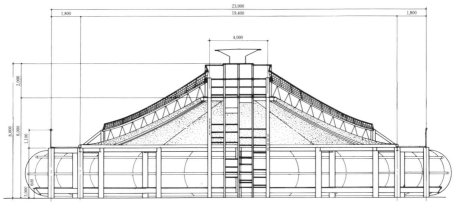

Fig. 2.33 Section of the Giant Tent play structure.

Fig. 2.34 The gate to the Giant Slope play structure 1. (*Photo: Fujitsuka Mitsumasa.*)

repeat, a circular play structure must have the following characteristics.

1. It must have a circulatory function.

2. It must allow children to experience a variety of challenges.

3. It must contain symbolic points.

4. It must allow children to experience "dizziness."

Fig. 2.35 The gate to the Giant Slope play structure 1. (*Photo: Fujitsuka Mitsumasa.*)

Fig. 2.36 Giant Slope play structure 2. The sloping floor is sufficient in itself to stimulate children. (*Photo: Fujitsuka Mitsumasa.*)

Fig. 2.37 Giant Slope play structure 2. A protruding deck. (*Photo: Fujitsuka Mitsumasa.*)

Fig. 2.38 Giant Slope play structure 2. A variety of handholds are attached to the sloping floor. (*Photo: Fujitsuka Mitsumasa.*)

5. It must have both large and small gathering places.

6. It must contain shortcuts.

7. It must have a "porous" structure.

"Circulation"

This was the first structure devised as a circular play structure. It comprises a 6 m by 6 m square and is made of wooden panels. (See Figs. 2.43 and 2.44.)

"G Play Structure"

This is a wooden circular play structure in the shape of a G. It was placed in the courtyard of a community center. (See Figs. 2.45 to 2.47.)

"Fortress of Winds"

The "Fortress of Winds" was constructed in a park overlooking Lake Suwa at an altitude of

Fig. 2.39 Giant Slope play structure 2. (*Photo: Fujitsuka Mitsumasa.*)

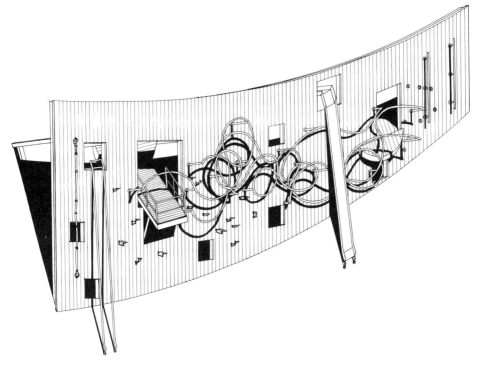

Fig. 2.40 Giant Slope play structure 2. Axonometric projection.

Fig. 2.41 Giant Earth play structure consisting of white logs placed on 2.5-m-high mounds of earth. (*Photo: Yutaka Suzuki.*)

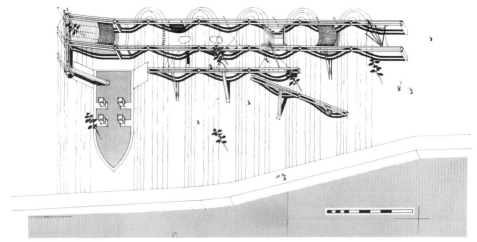

Fig. 2.42 Giant Earth play structure. Axonometric projection.

Fig. 2.43 Circulation. A typical 6-m-square circular play structure consisting of four columns, bridges connecting the columns, and a soft floor in the middle. (*Photo: Yoshio Shiratori.*)

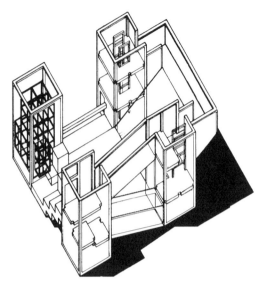

Fig. 2.44 Circulation. Axonometric projection.

1000 m. Inside the "Fortress of Winds," aspects of nature, such as the refreshing winds which bring in the seasons and the occasional turbulent whirlwinds, are expressed in curves, slopes, twists, and spirals. The path is made up of floorboards 2 m in width. It was designed to take in the natural undulation of the ground and has a circumference of 170 m. (See Figs. 2.48 to 2.52.)

Fig. 2.45 G Play Structure. (*Photo: Fujitsuka Mitsumasa.*)

Fig. 2.46 G Play Structure. The small circles stimulate children's play (*Photo: Fujitsuka Mitsumasa.*)

"Möbius Band"

A Möbius band is a long strip, usually of paper, which is given one twist and connected back onto itself. This play structure which has no front or back symbolizes play without end. (See Figs. 2.53 and 2.54.)

"Orbic"

This is a small circular play structure composed of two circles (Fig. 2.55). It is wooden, and the length of the circle is 20 m. It was designed mainly for small children and contains an outer circle which they can run

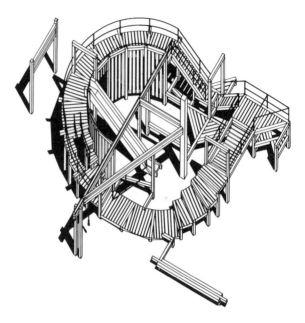

Fig. 2.47 G Play Structure. Axonometric projection.

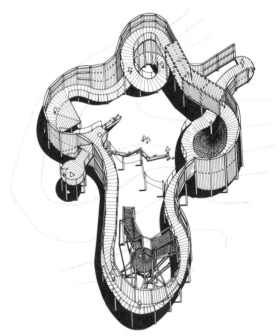

Fig. 2.48 Fortress of Winds. Axonometric projection. The concept of the circular play system materialized in the form of a giant fortress.

Fig. 2.49 Sloping floor of the Fortress of Winds. (*Photo: Fujitsuka Mitsumasa.*)

Fig. 2.50 Fortress of Winds. The 360-m-long wooden fortress with a view of Lake Suwa in the background. (*Photo: Fujitsuka Mitsumasa.*)

Fig. 2.51 Bridge of the Fortress of Winds. (*Photo: Fujitsuka Mitsumasa.*)

around, an inner circle rich in variety, and a net route for shortcuts.

"Running Circuit"

This is a play structure designed to allow children to run around to their hearts' content

Fig. 2.52 Fortress of Winds. Floor for children to run around on. (*Photo: Fujitsuka Mitsumasa.*)

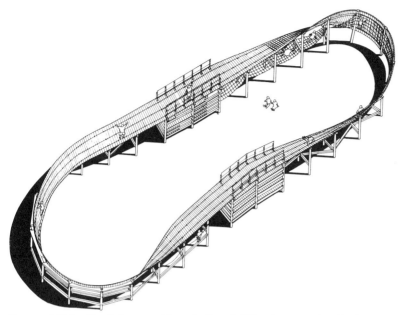

Fig. 2.53 Möbius Band. Axonometric projection. A 180-m-long wooden structure.

(Figs. 2.56 to 2.58). A huge wooden deck pathway 2 m in width and 400 m in length was designed to give the impression of an overhead expressway and sits on a 2500-square`2-Dmeter site. The slope, varying in height from 2.5 to 3.5 m above the ground, forms an endless road where children can run around as much as they want.

"Maze Place"

This is a simple maze made of wooden panels with gaps in between which make children lose their sense of perspective (Figs. 2.59 and 2.60). The parents can keep an eye on their children while they are inside the maze.

Community Play Structures

The twelve play structures named "community play structures" were designed for mass production, or in other words were created as industrial designs. Most of these

Fig. 2.54 Möbius Band. The twisted floor is sufficient in itself to provide a challenge for children (*Photo: Fujitsuka Mitsumasa.*)

Fig. 2.55 Orbic. Small circulations in a double spiral. (*Photo: Fujitsuka Mitsumasa.*)

were produced commercially by Kotobuki Corporation, a Japanese furniture maker. There are two basic concepts. One is that of a play structure designed for group play. On the whole, play structures in playgrounds in Japan have traditionally been structures for developing children's mobility, such as single-function slides and swings. These were evaluated from the point of view of how they would help children develop mobility and physical strength, while my play structures should be evaluated from the point of view of how they contribute to their group formation.

The second concept is their aesthetic value. The structures on which children play must also be pleasing to the eye. Play structures must be public art just like sculptures.

"Escargot"

This is a 20-m-long tube created out of straight and curved fiber-reinforced plastic

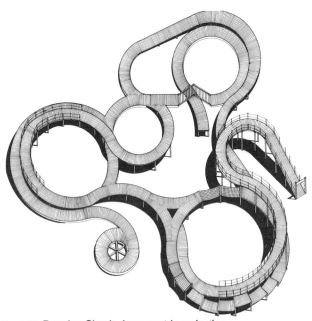

Fig. 2.56 Running Circuit. Axonometric projection.

(FRP) cylinders 60 cm in diameter (Fig. 2.61). There are holes in two places through which children can come out of the tube. Weaker children will not be able to climb to the top and will be "rescued" through a hole on the way. You can watch and talk to the children inside the tube from the outside.

"Ping Pong"

This is a tunnel play structure made by joining together semitransparent FRP spheres 1 m in diameter (Figs. 2.62, 2.63, and 2.64). Since the walls are semitransparent, parents can watch the children inside, giving a feeling of security to both the parents outside and the children inside. The semitransparent tunnel is made up of these spheres and provides a variety of spaces with different shades of light. There are also sections where other children disappear around corners and with wide and narrow as well as high and low places, all of which expand the imagination

Fig. 2.57 Running Circuit. You cannot stay on the floor unless you keep running. (*Photo: Fujitsuka Mitsumasa.*)

Fig. 2.58 Running Circuit. An endless floor to run on. (*Photo: Fujitsuka Mitsumasa.*)

Fig. 2.59 Maze place. The slits remove the sense of perspective. (*Photo: Fujitsuka Mitsumasa.*)

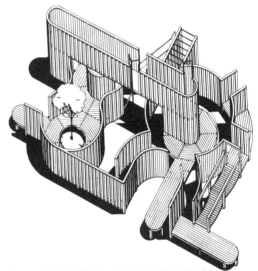

Fig. 2.60 Maze Place. Axonometric projection.

Fig. 2.61 Escargot. Semitransparent FRP tubes.

Fig. 2.62 Ping Pong. Shapes which bring back memories. (*Photo: Fujitsuka Mitsumasa.*)

Fig. 2.63 Ping Pong. There is something animal-like in the space inside the semitransparent FRP tubes. (*Photo: Fujitsuka Mitsumasa.*)

Fig. 2.64 Ping Pong. Axonometric projection.

Fig. 2.65 Cosmos. A combination of a jungle gym and soft cloth. (*Photo: Fujitsuka Mitsumasa.*)

Fig. 2.66 Cosmos. There is a soft hiding place inside the canvas. (*Photo: Fujitsuka Mitsumasa.*)

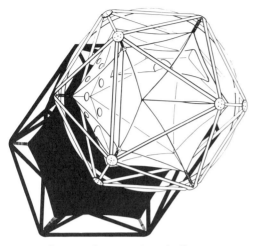

Fig. 2.67 Cosmos. Axonometric projection.

Fig. 2.68 Abacus Slider on a 10° slope. (*Photo: Yoshio Shiratori.*)

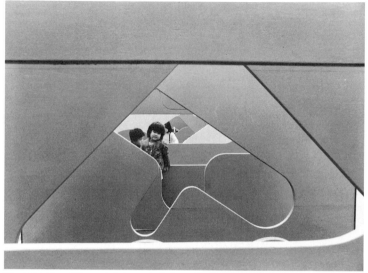

Fig. 2.69 Panel Tunnel. A tunnel of signs. (*Photo: Yoshio Shiratori.*)

of children at play. "Ping Pong" can be joined to the "Escargot" mentioned above.

"Cosmos"

The canvas capsule of this play structure (Figs. 2.65, 2.66, and 2.67) is supported by a twenty-sided pipe frame. The length of one

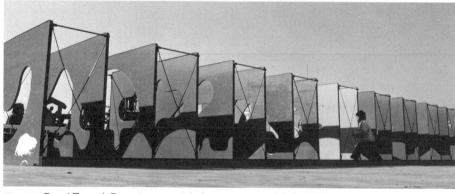

Fig. 2.70 Panel Tunnel. Parents can watch the movement of their children from the sidelines. (*Photo: Yoshio Shiratori.*)

Fig. 2.71 The House of Winds—a small play structure. (*Photo: Fujitsuka Mitsumasa.*)

side is 1.2 m and the height of the entire model is 2 m. One of the summits of the canvas capsule has been removed to create a hollow at the top which provides an open gathering spot for children and provides for the "rest" element of play. The structure is designed also to encourage dynamic play in which children can slide down from the top and jump into the inside of the capsule through a slit in the canvas. The inside of the canvas is a soft nestlike space.

"Abacus Slider"

This is a slide in the form of a polyethylene abacus. The vibration and noise generated when the children slide down on top of the huge abacus beads increase the sense of "dizziness" and expand and stimulate the children's imagination. The gradient is small, since with plastic rollers it is possible to slide even at an angle of 10°, and this is a safe structure especially for younger children. Children can slide down in a variety of ways, on cardboard and rubber mats or with three to

Fig. 2.72 The House of Winds. Axonometric projection.

Fig. 2.73 Sky Net. You can climb up the funnel-shaped net from the middle (*Photo: Yoshio Shiratori.*)

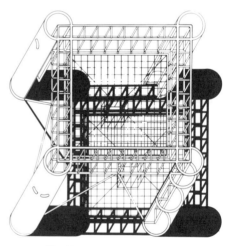

Fig. 2.74 Sky Net. Axonometric projection.

four children joining their hands together. (See Fig. 2.68.)

"Panel Tunnel"

This is a simple play structure in which panels with holes of different sizes in them are set parallel to each other to create a visual cave. This is a cave for small children, especially those who have just begun to walk, to explore. Parents need simply to watch their children from one side. Each panel is 1.6 m by 2.4 m. (See Figs. 2.69 and 2.70.)

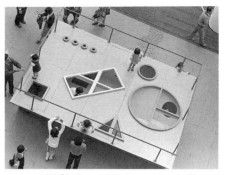

Fig. 2.75 W Station. A W-shaped boat with a three-dimensional maze inside. (*Photo: Yoshio Shiratori.*)

"House of Winds"

The "House of Winds" was developed as a structure for making possible a variety of games in relatively small spaces under 100 square meters, for example, in small playgrounds, courtyards on housing estates, small preschools, as well as in private homes. Its size is 2.7 m (length) by 1.5 m (width) by 2.4 m (height) and it can be constructed easily by assembling the prefabricated parts. The "House of Winds" contains a swing, a slide, a playhouse, a sandpit, a pole, and a basket hoop. The ladder swing can be replaced by flying rings, horizontal bars, and sandbags and the structure can also be used for exercise by other members of the family. (See Figs. 2.71 and 2.72.)

"Sky Net"

A net is hung, so as to form a funnel, from four pipe frame columns at a height of about 2 m. Each side is 4 to 5 m long. Children swing themselves on the net, jump onto the nets, climb up the columns, walk around the bars on the outside, and try climbing up the net from the center. An outstanding feature of this structure is the floating sensation children can have when throwing themselves onto the net. (See Figs. 2.73 and 2.74.)

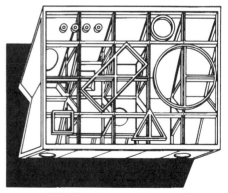

Fig. 2.76 W Station. Axonometric projection.

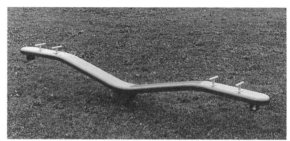

Fig. 2.77 Bird Seesaw. An FRP seesaw in the shape of a bird's wings. (*Photo: Kotobuki Corporation.*)

Fig. 2.78 Red House. A house for small children. (*Photo: Fujitsuka Mitsumasa.*)

Fig. 2.79 Red Shoe. A huge red shoe with a series of 60-cm-square spaces inside. (*Photo: Fujitsuka Mitsumasa.*)

"W Station"

This structure has the form of a W-shaped boat and is divided into several small rooms inside. There is a hole in the deck, and the whole comprises a three-dimensional maze. (See Figs. 2.75 and 2.76.)

"Bird Seesaw"

This is a seesaw made from molded plastic. Although seesaws are classic play structures, there are often problems regarding safety. The "Bird Seesaw" has the shape of bird's wings, with all the details rounded off, and is designed to be safe even when handled roughly by children (Fig. 2.77).

Playhouse—"Red House"

This device was designed under the concept that children's play structures should be like houses. The structure is basically a red house with a clearly defined chimney. It is divided into a number of small rooms, each having different shapes and sizes, and the whole comprises a mazelike space (Fig. 2.78).

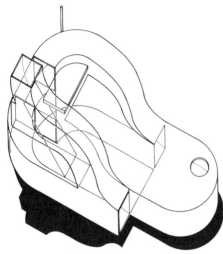

Fig. 2.80 Red Shoe. Axonometric projection.

Fig. 2.81 Möbius Ring. A commercially produced Möbius ring. (*Photo: Fujitsuka Mitsumasa.*)

Fig. 2.82 Tubie I. A slide dynamically encased by rings. (*Photo: Fujitsuka Mitsumasa.*)

"Red Shoe"

This is a structure centering around the experience of traveling through a 60-cm-square tunnel, which has variation in light and space. The hardness of the materials is counterbalanced by inclusion of curved sections to produce a strange formation. The contrast between the gentle slope and the cave was seen to help in the development of children's play activities. (See Figs. 2.79 and 2.80.)

"Möbius Ring"

The Möbius ring has been made into a ladder-form play structure using steel pipes (see Fig. 2.81).

"Tubie I"

This is a slide having as its basis a huge ring bent in two (see Figs. 2.82 and 2.83).

"Tubie II"

This play structure is intended to give the impression of a yellow space ship. The inside forms a playhouse. It is a structure for active play with slides and sliding bars (see Figs. 2.84 and 2.85).

"Super Log"

Logs are bound together while being made to stagger slightly and the entire structure is made to form a distorted ring. A net is also attached to give variety in the types of games which can be played. (See Figs. 2.86 and 2.87.)

"Big Horn"

This is a play structure in the form of a voice tube and has an odd visual effect. (See Figs. 2.88 and 2.89.)

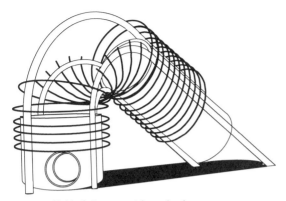

Fig. 2.83 Tubie I. Axonometric projection.

Fig. 2.84 Tubie II. (*Photo: Fujitsuka Mitsumasa.*)

Fig. 2.85 Tubie II. The interior with the atmosphere of a space station. (*Photo: Fujitsuka Mitsumasa.*)

Fig. 2.86 Super Log. A play structure made of logs joined at skewed angles. It looks unstable at first sight. (*Photo: Fujitsuka Mitsumasa.*)

Environment Discovery Play Structures

I was commissioned to design the Children's Plaza for the Tsukuba Science Expo in 1985. This gave me the opportunity to begin developing play structures designed to help children learn about their environment while playing, about the workings of the environment which are not obvious to the eye, for example, by sensing light, sound, and winds and listening to sounds which have

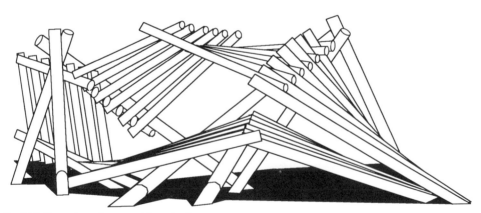

Fig. 2.87 Super Log. Axonometric projection.

Fig. 2.88 Big Horn. One finds out which tube is connected with which by shouting into one tube and listening into others. (*Photo: Fujitsuka Mitsumasa.*)

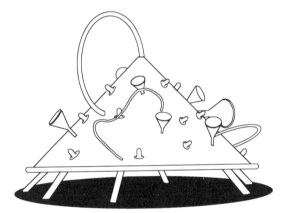

Fig. 2.89 Big Horn. Axonometric projection.

Fig. 2.90 Tsukuba Expo Children's Plaza. Distorted Space. (*Photo: Fujitsuka Mitsumasa.*)

Fig. 2.91 Tsukuba Expo Children's Plaza. Distorted Space. (*Photo: Fujitsuka Mitsumasa.*)

been magnified. These are often listed separately as outdoor versions of devices for science museums, but they were basically conceived of as being elements of the play environment.

Play Structures at the Tsukuba Expo Children's Plaza

An expo on the theme of scientific technology was held in the Tsukuba Academic New Town, 50 km to the north of

Fig. 2.92 Tsukuba Expo Children's Plaza. Trompe l'Oeil Wood. (*Design collaboration: Shigeo Fukuda. Photo: Fujitsuka Mitsumasa.*)

Fig. 2.93 Tsukuba Expo Children's Plaza. Mechanimal Pond. (*Photo: Fujitsuka Mitsumasa.*)

Fig. 2.94 Tsukuba Expo Children's Plaza. Parabola Talk. (*Design collaboration: Sekkeikobo. Photo: Fujitsuka Mitsumasa.*)

Tokyo, in 1985. An area of 3 ha at the center of the 100-ha site was designated the "Children's Plaza" and devoted to play structures on which children could "experience science" while playing on them.

"Distorted Space." This formed the entrance to the Children's Plaza, an open space with modified perspective, an outdoor version of the distorted room (see Figs. 2.90 and 2.91).

"Trompe l'Oeil Wood." Animals were depicted in a wood made of white L-shaped steel bars. Children can see animals when they stand in a certain viewpoint (Fig. 2.92). Children can

Fig. 2.95 Tsukuba Expo Children's Plaza. Maze of Doors. (*Photo: Fujitsuka Mitsumasa.*)

Fig. 2.96 Wonder Plaza at the Central Children's Land. Surrounded by lawns and trees.

Fig. 2.97 Wonder Plaza at the Central Children's Land.

Fig. 2.98 Wonder Plaza at the Central Children's Land. The rubber floor draws new kinds of play out of children.

also play hide and seek in the wood.

"Mechanimal Pond"—Mechanicars. This is a ride representing as faithfully as possible the movement of insects, which children can move either by remote control or by pushing with their feet (Fig. 2.93).

"Parabola Talk." Children can talk to each other over a distance using a parabolic antenna (Fig. 2.94).

"Maze of Doors." This is a maze made out of doors which have hidden information on them (Fig. 2.95). The doors have been designed as a play structure for providing information.

"Wonder Plaza" at the Central Children's Land

Central Children's Land was constructed on a 100-ha site on the outskirts of Tokyo in 1965 to commemorate the marriage of the present emperor of Japan, then the crown prince.

In 1990, a special corner was created in the park where children could discover and enjoy nature while playing (Figs. 2.96, 2.97, 2.98, and 2.99). The themes are sound, light, and wind. Fish-eye lenses, colored glass, telescopic lenses, a small planetarium, a parabolic antenna for listening to the birds, and the wind and voice tubes are dotted around the area. We hoped that children would be able to magnify their perception

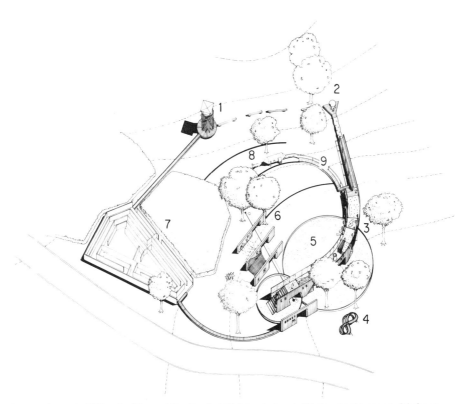

Fig. 2.99 Layout of Wonder Plaza at the Central Children's Land: (1) Tower of Lenses, (2) Open Planetarium, (3) main deck, (4) Möbius Ring, (5) sand pit , (6) Main Panels, (7) jungle gym (8) Echo Tube, (9) voice tube.

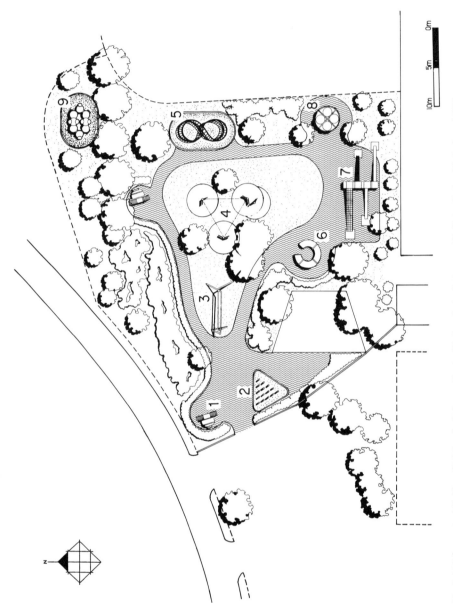

Fig. 2.100 Layout of Beijing Children's Science Park: (1) Parabola Antenna, (2) Color Pole, (3) Swing, (4)Mirror Panel, (5) Möbius Ring, (6) Echo Tube, (7) Friction Slider, (8) Magic Eye, (9) Ping Pong.

Fig. 2.101 Beijing Children's Science Park. Echo Tube.

Fig. 2.102 Beijing Children's Science Park. Magic Eye.

Fig. 2.103 Beijing Children's Science Park. Mirror Panel.

Fig. 2.104 Beijing Children's Science Park. Friction Slider.

and enjoy the natural environment while they were playing.

Play Structures at the Beijing Children's Science Park

These structures were constructed adjacent to the Beijing Children's Science Museum which is located within the Yuantan Park in Beijing. There are nine of these scientific

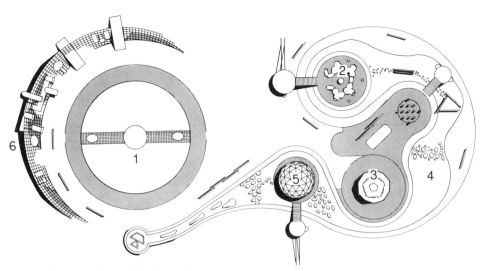

Fig. 2.105 Layout of Space World Fun-Fun Kids: (1) Space Shooter, (2) Space Bubble, (3) Space Tube, (4) Space River, (5) Fog Capsule, (6) Space Jungle.

Fig. 2.106 Space World Fun-Fun Kids. Space Tube. (*Photo: Fujitsuka Mitsumasa.*)

Fig. 2.107 Space World Fun-Fun Kids. Space Tube. Pipes 1 m in diameter are combined to make a 6-m-high dodecahedron. (*Photo: Fujitsuka Mitsumasa.*)

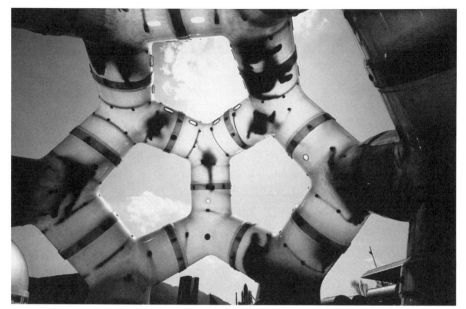

Fig. 2.108 Space World Fun-Fun Kids. Space Tube. (*Photo: Fujitsuka Mitsumasa.*)

play structures in all. Four of them are discussed here (Figs. 2.100 to 2.104).

"Echo Tube." A device for learning through experience about the resonation of sound and voice.

"Magic Eye." A device for visual experience showing how the scenery changes when

Fig. 2.109 Space World Fun-Fun Kids. Space Shooter. Mt. Fuji made of canvas, creating a soft slide. (*Photo: Fujitsuka Mitsumasa.*)

Fig. 2.110 Space World Fun-Fun Kids. Space River. Children love playing with water. The dodecahedron tubes can be seen on the left. (*Photo: Fujitsuka Mitsumasa.*)

viewed through different lenses.

"Mirror Panel." A device for learning through experience the various principles of the angles of incidence and reflection using mobile bells.

"Friction Slider." A device for learning through experience about friction resistance using four slides.

"Space World Fun-Fun Kids"

This was an amusement park with a space theme built by Nippon Steel Corporation, Japan's top steel manufacturer. We were commissioned to design a playground for small children at the center of the park. The site comprises a complex of play structures for environment discovery through sensations of water, wind, sound, and light (see Figs. 2.105 to 2.112).

"Space Tube." Here, the children pass through a three-dimensional maze made up of Y-shaped cylindrical tubes. The structure as a whole forms a regular dodecahedron with a diameter of 6 m.

"Space Shooter." Children slide down in all directions on a large tent, 4 m high and 19 m

Fig. 2.111 Space World Fun-Fun Kids. Space Jungle. (*Photo: Fujitsuka Mitsumasa.*)

Fig. 2.112 Space World Fun-Fun Kids. Space Jungle. (*Photo: Fujitsuka Mitsumasa.*)

Fig. 2.113 Yokaichi Rampart Park. A mound with fortress-like walls. (*Photo: Tomio Ohashi.*)

Fig. 2.114 Yokaichi Rampart Park. A tunnel inside the mound. (*Photo: Tomio Ohashi.*)

Fig. 2.115 Yokaichi Rampart Park. Play structure devices on the walls. (*Photo: Tomio Ohashi.*)

Fig. 2.116 Yokaichi Rampart Park. A bridge penetrating the wall. (*Photo: Tomio Ohashi.*)

Fig. 2.117 Yokaichi Rampart Park. (*Photo: Tomio Ohashi.*)

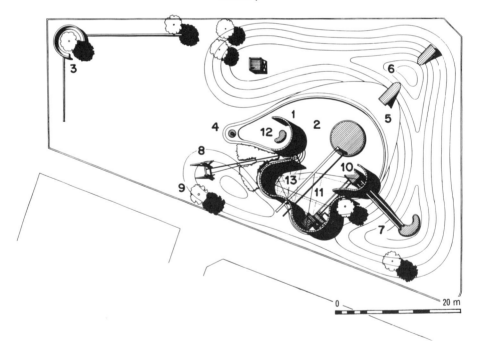

Fig. 2.118 Layout of Yokaichi Rampart Park. A small hill and the sky: (1) Castle wall, (2) sand pit, (3) bench circle, (4) water tap, (5) slider, (6) tunnel, (7) net bridge, (8) swing, (9) vegetation, (10) tower, (11) gate, (12) stage, (13) rope.

in diameter, rather like the tent at a circus.

"Space River." This is a shallow 600-square-meter pool 10 cm deep for use of small children.

"Space Bubble." This device is for creating a large amount of soap bubbles every hour on the hour.

Landscape Play Structures

What I call "landscape play structures" are basically structures for exciting play in children, but they have as another more important function that of providing a landmark in the play environment. These are closely related to outdoor sculptures as public art but are different in that they have as their ultimate aim enticing children to play.

Yokaichi Rampart Park. This 700-square-meter park was constructed in the middle of a new housing estate. A 4-m-high block wall with undulating sides, along with a wooden viewing tower, circular stage, net bridge,

Fig. 2.119 Kaminoyama Children's Park. Mound, wall, and tube. (*Photo: Fujitsuka Mitsumasa.*)

Fig. 2.120 Kaminoyama Children's Park. A wooden jungle gym stuck into the side of a hill. (*Photo: Fujitsuka Mitsumasa.*)

Fig. 2.121 Kaminoyama Children's Park. An FRP tube coming out of the undulating wooden play structure. (*Photo: Fujitsuka Mitsumasa.*)

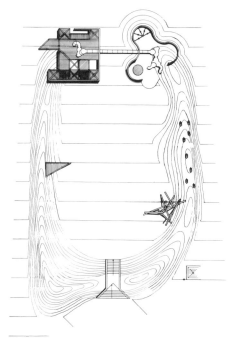

Fig. 2.122 Layout of the Kaminoyama Children's Park. A portal play structure with the undulating mounds surrounding the open space in the middle.

white concrete slide, tunnel, and lawn, none of which are particularly functional as play structures on their own, but the area as a whole has been designed as a high-density playground providing all the necessary functions for active play. (See Figs. 2.113 to 2.118.)

Kaminoyama Children's Park. This park too is not particularly large (1000 square meters). An open space surrounded by a row of mounds, wooden undulating wall, FRP pipe bridge, and wooden deck, which together comprise a fortress for children to play in. (See Figs. 2.119 to 2.122.)

Tachinoura Park in Kita-Kyushu. The old harbor at Kita-Kyushu was reclaimed as a result of the changes in methods of handling cargo to give way to a new port. This park was constructed as a part of a chain of parks on the newly reclaimed site. Since the surrounding area is not residential, this park was designed mainly as a place for the local

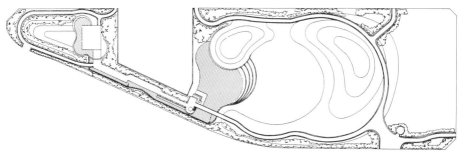

Fig. 2.123 Layout of Tachinoura Park in Kita-Kyushu. Area: 5540 square meters.

residents to visit on holidays. An attempt was made to create a park where the citizens of Kita-Kyushu and their children could relax in a landscape which goes beyond the ordinary human scale. (See Figs. 2.123 to 2.129.)

*Mikumayama Park.*Recreational facilities have been constructed for the local residents and tourists on a hill called Mikumayama, located to the south of Sumoto, the largest city on Awaji Island, in the Inland Sea of Japan. (See Figs. 2.130 and 2.131.) The several play structures constructed here were designed also to enhance the scenery.

DESIGN OF ROADS FOR CHILDREN

Roads used in the past to be playgrounds for children. When the first survey on children's playing environments was conducted in Japan in Osaka by a landscape architect by the name of Reijo Oya in 1924, it was found that the majority of children played on the streets rather than in parks. Oya made a proposal for changing the structure of roads to allow children to play safely on them. Schools began, however, to forbid children to play on roads after World War II. This was largely because of the rapid increase in road accidents with the increase in traffic from the

Fig. 2.124 Tachinoura Park in Kita-Kyushu. Revitalizing a stream.

Fig. 2.125 Tachinoura Park in Kita-Kyushu.

Fig. 2.126 Tachinoura Park in Kita-Kyushu.

1950s onward, especially on the narrow roads and streets of Japan.

The number of deaths of children in traffic accidents reached its peak in the 1960s. This led to the separation of walkways on the roads in Japan, but in recent years a review of the situation has been proposed by those who maintain that the separation of the functions of roads has taken the enjoyment out of roads and made them less human. It is the mingling of hawkers, horses, dogs, bicycles, and cars that make streets a fun place to be. It is not possible to have such a situation on all streets, but people began to think in the 1980s that there might perhaps be a case for having a mix of cars and pedestrians, as well as areas for children to play in, at least on minor roads.

According to our study in Yokohama, areas where children play in residential areas can be classified into three types, the roads themselves, narrow streets with bulges in them, and areas adjacent to roads, the latter two also being areas intimately connected

Fig. 2.127 Tachinoura Park in Kita-Kyushu. (*Photo: Fujitsuka Mitsumasa.*)

with roads. For a road to be a place where children can play the volume of traffic must be less than 30 vehicles per hour and the cars going through must be traveling at speeds below 10 km/h. It is possible to reduce the volume and speed of traffic to below these limits, so as to create roads where children can play.

Although the examples given below of roads I have designed do not include mixed roads, they were designed along similar concepts. They may be called large walkways, which have been designed with children's play as the main themes.

Fig. 2.128 Tachinoura Park in Kita-Kyushu.

Old Tamagawa Waterway Promenade. Box culverts for the underground railway pass 60 cm below this path, while adjacent to it are two trunk roads, which form parts of the Koshu Highway and the Metropolitan Expressway, which provided a particularly unsatisfactory environment around the pathway despite its location in a residential

Fig. 2.129 Tachinoura Park in Kita-Kyushu.

Fig. 2.130 Mikumayama Park. Viewpoint play structure "Endless Earth." (*Photo: Fujitsuka Mitsumasa.*)

Fig. 2.131 Mikumayama Park. Wooden play structure "Into Space." (*Photo: Fujitsuka Mitsumasa.*)

Fig. 2.132 Old Tamagawa Waterway Promenade. The path is situated along one of the busiest trunk roads in Japan. The presence of water is a big attraction for children. (*Photo: Fujitsuka Mitsumasa.*)

Fig. 2.133 Old Tamagawa Waterway Promenade. (*Photo: Fujitsuka Mitsumasa.*)

area. The total length of the footpath is 3.7 km, of which 400 m was newly constructed. There are a primary school and a preschool along the path. The new 400-m section was divided into three blocks, the promenade block, school and preschool block, and stream block (see Figs. 2.132 to 2.138). In the last of these, 120 m in length, the streams of water flowing from sculptures completely have changed the unsatisfactory atmosphere of the area and attract a large number of children who come to play here. A corner was devoted to children's play structures in the school and preschool block.

Mikasa Park Approach Road in Yokosuka. Yokosuka is a town south of Yokohama with an American navy base. The municipal government is planning to build a 10-km footpath along the beach, and the Mikasa Park Approach Road, constructed by

Fig. 2.134 Old Tamagawa Waterway Promenade. Children love running water. (*Sculptor: Aijiro Wakita. Photo: Fujitsuka Mitsumasa.*)

Fig. 2.135 Old Tamagawa Waterway Promenade. A forestlike play structure for small children. (*Photo: Fujitsuka Mitsumasa.*)

Fig. 2.136 Old Tamagawa Waterway Promenade. (*Photo: Fujitsuka Mitsumasa.*)

renovating the 300-m access road leading from the navy base to a park by the sea, is to provide a model section for this project (see Figs. 2.139 to 2.141). There used to be carriageways on either side of a green belt in the middle. The carriageway was limited to one side and the other was turned into a 26-m-wide footpath, with a small stream flowing through the whole to provide a place where children could play in water.

"Play Road Stations." Floats are an indispensable part of festivals in Japan. Symbols of deities are carried around the streets by people on these floats, turning the streets on which they are passing into festive spaces. The "Play Road Stations" have no religious significance but are floats (mobile devices) which temporarily turn the streets into spaces for children to play in. (See Figs. 2.142 to 2.144.)

Fig. 2.137 Old Tamagawa Waterway Promenade. Curved benches along a straight path. (*Photo: Fujitsuka Mitsumasa.*)

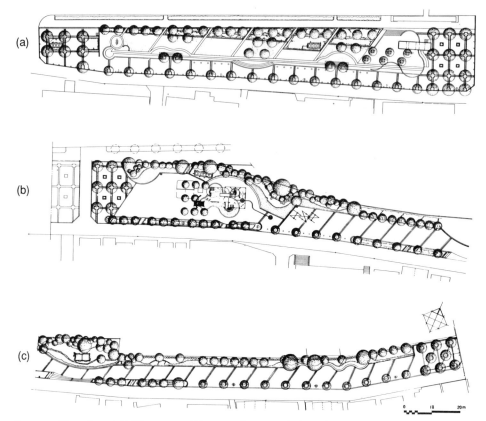

(a)

(b)

(c)

Fig. 2.138 Plan view of Old Tamagawa Waterway Promenade. Length: 400 m, average width: 18 m. (*a*) Stream block; (*b*) block adjoining municipal offices, kindergarten and primary school, with exhaust towers for the underground railway; (*c*) the path extends westward from Hatsudai Station on the Keio Line. There is a row of office buildings on the northern side of the path.

Fig. 2.139 Mikasa Park Approach Road in Yokosuka. (*Photo: Fujitsuka Mitsumasa.*)

Fig. 2.140 Mikasa Park Approach Road in Yokosuka. (*Photo: Fujitsuka Mitsumasa.*)

"Cubic Stations." These stations are positioned by the side of the pedestrian malls in shopping areas. Children can play and wait for their parents here while they are shopping (Fig. 2.145).

CONDITIONS FOR PLAYGROUNDS

I would first like to make a bold definition that good playgrounds are those where people gather and second, they must at the same time be beautiful parks. Parks where people gather have something which attract them there, while parks which do not attract people

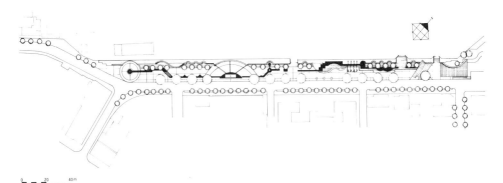

Fig. 2.141 Mikasa Park Approach Road in Yokosuka. A 300-m street has been laid out between the American Navy base and the sea at Yokosuka.

must have something that deters them from gathering there.

Playgrounds by nature are collections of fairly undefined spaces, while playing is a collection of undefined actions. The capacities for and tastes in play differ according to the ages of the children. Capacity for movement, physical strength, and objects of interest vary according to a child's age and sex. There is a need to cater to the various activities of the users of the parks, but it is not desirable to classify parks according to users, into those for young children, for teenagers, and for the elderly, or

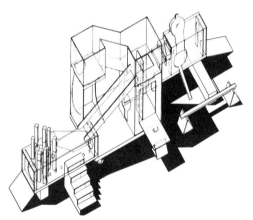

Fig. 2.142 Play Road Stations. Axonometric projection.

Fig. 2.143 Play Road Stations. (*Photo: Fujitsuka Mitsumasa.*)

Fig. 2.144 Play Road Stations. The unit can be assembled easily by children. (*Photo: Fujitsuka Mitsumasa.*)

Fig. 2.145 Cubic Station. A base for play situated on a shopping street. (*Photo: Fujitsuka Mitsumasa.*)

according to genres such as athletic parks, scenic parks, and sculpture parks. Activities in parks are by nature ambiguous, and someone who originally came to a park to play, for example, may end up jogging there. Users do not use parks for singular purposes.

SPATIAL COMPOSITION OF PLAYGROUNDS

Play in open spaces may be classified largely into (1) ball games like baseball and soccer,

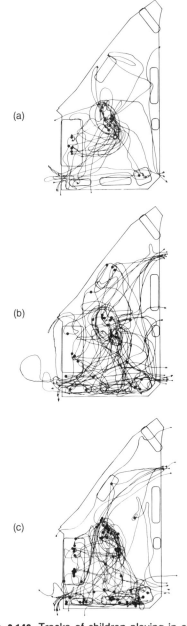

(a)

(b)

(c)

Fig. 2.146 Tracks of children playing in a park: (*a*) six children (four boys and two girls), one- to three-year-olds; (*b*) twelve children (seven boys and five girls), four- to six-year-olds; (*c*) fourteen children (six boys and eight girls), seven- to twelve-year-olds.

(2) contact games like tag and (3) imitation games like playing at housekeeping. The amount of space required differs according to these categories. Ball games require 300 to 1500 square meters, contact games require 150 to 1000 square meters, and imitation games 60 to 300 square meters.

The outer limits of the space are an important element in open-space playgrounds. In a study on playing fields I conducted in 1980, I found that open spaces were surrounded by roads, alleys, large trees, buildings, houses, and walls and these give an accent to the open space. Games like tag and hide-and-seek require trees, buildings, and walls children can hide behind around the open space in the middle. The open space in children's amusement grounds tends to be surrounded by vegetation and play structures rather than by buildings like warehouses.

Parks with too many play structures and almost no open space are fine for small children of preschool age to play in but not for larger children of primary school age. Once the children reach the top grades of primary school, their play becomes centered on ball games and contact games and play on play structures is limited to temporary intervals between other games. There must first be an open space in parks for these children and there should not be too many play structures or too much vegetation. An open space on its own, on the other hand, cannot provide for the variety required in play. Children constantly switch to new games. One moment they are playing a ball game, the next they are playing hide-and-seek or tag, and a few minutes later they may be moving onto the play structures. The open space must therefore be surrounded by play structures and vegetation. Figure 2.146 shows the paths of children playing in a park. The paths differ according to the ages of the children, and a close observation of the paths also reveals that there is a circular flow throughout the park. In other words, the open space and its periphery comprise a circular play system. A good playground will consist of large and small circular structures of play distributed around the ground like cells in a human body.

PLAY STRUCTURES AND OPEN SPACE

The relationship between play structures and open space in amusement grounds and playgrounds will greatly affect the patterns and development of children's play in them. A small amusement ground may consist either of an open space in the middle with play structures surrounding it or of a symbolic play structure in the middle with an open space surrounding it. In the former case, the open space in the middle of the park should have an area of at least around 150 square meters. The play structures in such cases tend to be single-function structures such as slides, swings, and jungle gyms. In terms of the circular play system, there should also be trees and vegetation around the open space for children to hide in. The play structures in such places should also include something in the nature of a play wall. In the case of an amusement ground with a play structure in the middle, the nature of that play structure is of importance. The structure should be a community play structure, that is, a giant play structure with a circular play system. In such cases too, the open space should have a certain unity and an area of at least about 120 square meters. The composition of the amusement ground will be determined by whether it is of the open-space-centered type or the play-structure-centered type, but in either case, it should have a circular play system and there must be a "porous" relationship between the play structures.

The relationship between play structures surrounding the open space will also be of importance (see Fig. 2.147). The play structures should be located at nodal points between the open spaces.

For children in the upper grades of primary school and above, it will suffice if play structures are dotted around the open space, but for smaller children the layout of the play structures is of greater importance than the open space, since these smaller children play more on the play structures than in the open space. In designing an amusement ground for small children, one must also consider the accompanying parents. If the play structures are too spread out, there is a danger of older children cycling around between them and colliding with the smaller children. Another problem is that accompanying adults will have to follow the children every time they move from one structure to another and this will hinder free

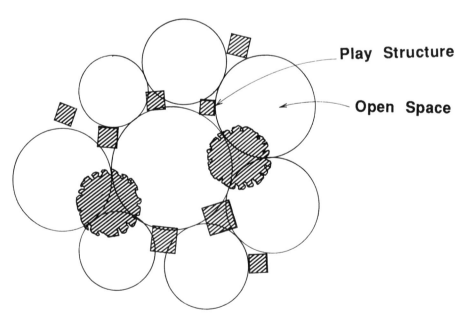

Play Structure

Open Space

Fig. 2.147 The figure shows the relationship between play structures and open spaces. The bubble-shaped open spaces are joined onto each other.

play on the part of the children. To cater to the needs of small children, a space should be set aside which is inaccessible to bicycles and where a number of play structures with different functions comprise a composite whole.

3 Theory and Design of "Parks" and Architecture for Children

SIX TYPES OF SPACES AS PLAY ENVIRONMENTS FOR CHILDREN

Observations made on children's play activities in 39 school districts in Japan in a study on children's play space indicate that the play space can be classified into six large categories. At one level, children's playgrounds can be classified into places such as school playgrounds, parks, temple grounds, and gardens but these merely indicate the physical locations and give no indication of what the children do there and how they play there. The six categories of play space listed below do not designate specific locations but represent the spaces as conceived by children.

Nature Spaces

Spaces endowed with trees, water, and living creatures are the spaces most basic and important to children's play.

Open Spaces

These are extensive spaces where children can run around to their hearts' content. They may be called playing fields. It is important for children that these spaces are large enough to accommodate the most energetic play activities.

Road Spaces

Before cars came to monopolize roads in

Japan, roads used to be the main playgrounds for children. Roads are where children meet each other and they serve as a network connecting various bases for play.

Adventure Spaces

These are spaces full of confusion, such as rubbish dumps and construction sites. They serve to stimulate children's imagination.

Hideout Spaces

I call hideout spaces the bases children make and keep secret from their parents and teachers. Children grow up through this experience of having independent spaces unknown to their parents and other adults.

Play Structure Spaces

These are spaces which have play structures as their medium. They will have a growing importance as places where play can be concentrated and as symbolic playgrounds.

FOUR TYPES OF "PARKS" FOR CHILDREN

What I call "parks" here are the large-scale facilities where children and their families can have fun, such as large amusement grounds and parks, theme parks, and leisure lands. My view is that there are four types of "parks" as play environments, according to what they offer for the enjoyment of their users.

"Parks" for Enjoyment of "Dizziness"

Most commercial amusement parks belong to this category. Roger Caillois, a French sociologist, defines "dizziness" as one of the four elements of play. The areas in this category are parks which have this "dizziness" as their theme.

"Parks" for Enjoyment of Nature

"Parks" for enjoyment of nature have elements of nature such as the sea, mountains, and rivers as their themes. They may be subdivided into "parks" where people enjoy nature without any artificial elements and those where nature has been given a certain amount of artificial modification.

"Parks" for Enjoyment of Stories

One of the four elements proposed by Caillois is "imitation." "Parks" which have this as their theme may be considered "parks" for the enjoyment of stories. They include Meiji Village in Japan, Skansen in Sweden, and the EPCOT Center in the United States.

"Parks" for Enjoyment of Discovery and Experience

By visiting these "parks," adults and children can discover things they have never seen or experienced before, and this experience in itself can provide sufficient enjoyment. These "parks" are designed centering around the form of play which involves positive efforts for experience, creativity, and discovery on the part of the users.

Central Children's Land

This park was opened in 1965. The overall master plan was by Takashi Asada, and I was asked to design five of the facilities and plazas (see Fig. 3.1). The park as a whole was designed as a "park" for enjoying artificially modified nature and covers an area of 100 ha. The five facilities I designed are as follows.

- Splash pond (Fig. 3.2)

- Children's Center and greenhouse (Figs. 3.3 and 3.4)

- Center House (Fig. 3.5)

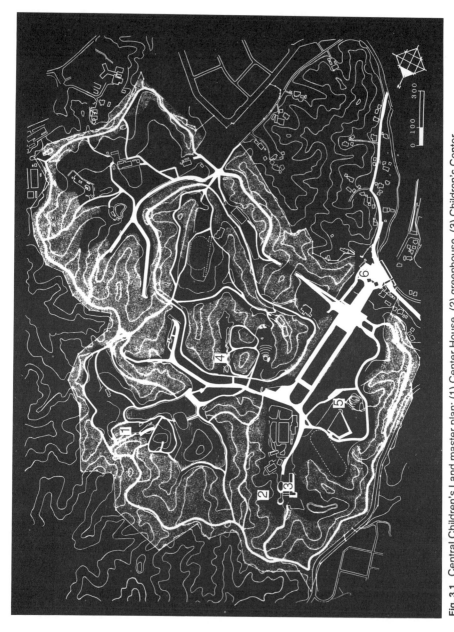

Fig. 3.1 Central Children's Land master plan: (1) Center House, (2) greenhouse, (3) Children's Center, (4)) splash pond, (5) Wonder Plaza, (6) office building.

Fig. 3.2 Central Children's Land. A pond with a natural spring. (*Photo: Fujitsuka Mitsumasa.*)

Fig. 3.3 Central Children's Land. Greenhouse and Children's Center.

Fig. 3.4 Central Children's Land. Greenhouse and Children's Center.

- Office building (Fig. 3.6)

- Environment discovery play structure (Figs. 3.7 and 3.8)

Atagoyama Children's Land

This park, opened in 1974, was built on a hill protruding like a peninsula into the city of Kofu, 100 km to the west of Tokyo. It has an area of 50 ha and a view over the city. It was designed as a "park" for the enjoyment of nature. The axis of flow was set at 425 m above sea level and the main road was built here with various facilities for outdoor activities for children, including a viewpoint square, branching off from it. (See Figs. 3.9 to 3.11.)

Sand Dunes Children's Land

This 13-ha park, set in a gently sloping Japanese black pine forest, was opened in 1973. Since the whole of the park is located within a designated nature park area, half of the buildings are buried underground. It was designed as a "park" where children could discover, experience, and create while enjoying nature. (See Figs. 3.12 and 3.13.)

Toriidaira Yamabiko Park

This 26-ha park was constructed on the slope of a hill by Lake Suwa in central Japan. There is natural variation in the topography with valleys and hillocks, as well as the added advantage of the view over Lake Suwa. (See Figs. 3.14 through 3.17.)

Mikumayama Park

This park, located in Sumoto on Awaji Island, has a relatively small area of 5.7 ha but is set in a scenic spot with views over the Inland Sea (see Figs. 3.18 and 3.19). It is divided into an "Open Space Zone" for multipurpose use and a "Nature Zone" where

Fig. 3.5 Center House at the Central Children's Land. (*Photo: Fujitsuka Mitsumasa.*)

Fig. 3.6 Office building at the Central Children's Land. (*Photo: Koji Murakoshi.*)

Fig. 3.7 Central Children's Land. Play structures in the Wonder Plaza. (*Photo: Fujitsuka Mitsumasa.*)

Fig. 3.8 Central Children's Land. Play structures in the Wonder Plaza. (*Photo: Fujitsuka Mitsumasa.*)

Fig. 3.9 Atagoyama Children's Land master plan: (1) Viewpoint plaza, (2) giant play structures, (3) Freedom Plaza, (4) House of Nature for Young People, (5) campsite.

Fig. 3.10 Atagoyama Children's Land. A view of the viewpoint plaza. (*Photo: Fujitsuka Mitsumasa.*)

Fig. 3.11 Atagoyama Children's Land. (*Photo: Fujitsuka Mitsumasa.*)

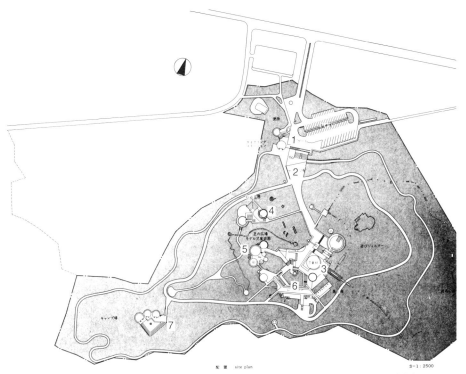

Fig. 3.12 Sand Dunes Children's Land master plan: (1) Entrance, (2) entrance plaza, (3) Children's Center, (4) workshop, (5) Sand Dunes Museum, (6) restaurant, (7) camp site.

Fig. 3.13 Sand Dunes Children's Land. An aerial view of the central area. (*Photo: Tomio Ohashi.*)

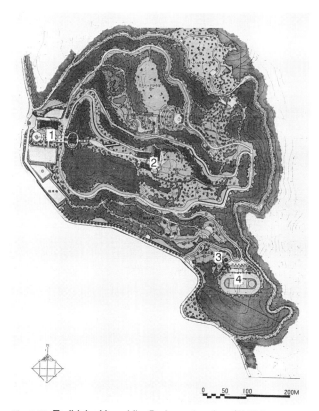

Fig. 3.14 Toriidaira Yamabiko Park master plan: (1) Entrance plaza, (2) center house, (3) Fortress of Winds, (4) roller-skating rink.

Fig. 3.15 Entrance to Toriidaira Yamabiko Park. (*Photo: Shoukokusha Publishing Co., Ltd.*)

Fig. 3.16 Toriidaira Yamabiko Park. Roller-skating rink. (*Photo: Fujitsuka Mitsumasa.*)

the natural environment is protected and which is designed mainly for people to take walks in. The site is varied in terms of topography as well as flora, and various devices for the enjoyment of nature are located along the footpaths, including two wooden giant play structures and two viewpoint play structures. It has been designed as a "diving board" from which to enjoy nature.

Tsukuba Expo Children's Plaza

A 3-ha area at the center of the site for the Science Expo held at Tsukuba in 1985 was designated the Children's Plaza and designed as a "park" for the enjoyment of discovery.

Fig. 3.17 Toriidaira Yamabiko Park. Park office. (*Photo: Fujitsuka Mitsumasa.*)

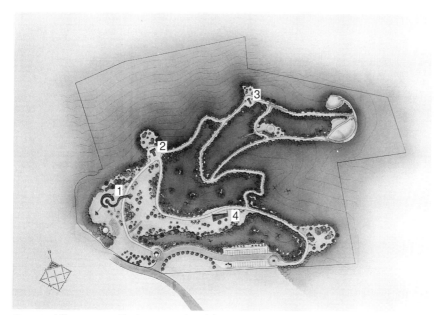

Fig. 3.18 Mikumayama Park master plan: (1) wooden play structure "Into Space," (2) wooden play structure "Endless Earth," (3) wooden play structure "To the Sea," (4) wooden play structure "To the Sky."

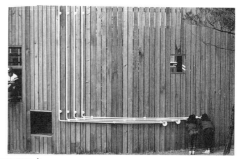

Fig. 3.19 Mikumayama Park. (*Photo: Fujitsuka Mitsumasa.*)

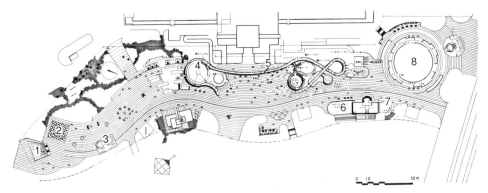

112 Chapter Three

Fig. 3.20 Tsukuba Expo Children's Plaza master plan: (1) Distorted Space, (2) Maze of Doors, (3) Trompe l'Oeil Wood, (4) Giant Tent play structure, (5) Fun Tube, (6) Mechanic Circus, (7) Mechanimal Pond, (8) Cosmoland.

Approximately 40 objects were dotted around the 3-ha site, including a scientific sculpture which made strange movements, a 300-m giant tube called the "Fun Tube," and a number of mechanical animals called "Mechanimals." Both adults and children could find fun and beauty here (see Figs. 3.20, 3.21, and 3.22).

The plaza was divided into three blocks. The first of these was the block nearest the central entrance called the "Garden of Wonders." This was an area where people could experience a strange microcosm, comprising a "Wonder Corridor" which created optical illusion and which might be called an outdoor version of the Distorted Room, a "Maze of Doors," a "Trompe l'Oeil Jungle," and a "Water Arch." The wonder corridor provided the entrance to this world. Eighty-five doors were used for the "Maze of Doors" which was meant to symbolize travel from one world to another.

The second block contained a "Fun Tube." This was a continuous play structure for scientific experience, with various devices located along a walkway 2.7 m in diameter, 1.8 m in width, and 270 m in length. The canvas slide called "Mountain Slider" provided a large shady area in the summer.

The third block was the "Earth and Mechanimal Zoo" Plaza, made up of "Animal Eyes," "Mechanicars," "Magnitude Floor" (an earthquake simulation device), and a model of Japan. For the model of Japan (diameter: 36 m, height: 2.6 m), the section of a 1/100,000 scale globe around Japan was reproduced in such a way that children could get a feel for the roundness of the earth.

The "Fun Tube" is an enlarged version of a type of play structure I had been producing. My method in designing play structures is to transform children's lines of movement into concrete objects. In doing so, one has to ensure that the flow lines themselves are fun and have variety and that the experience on them involves what Caillois calls "dizziness." Long tunnels, for example, are sufficient in themselves to arouse children's imagination.

Takebe no Mori Park

This 30-ha park, built in a joint development project between the local government and private enterprise, was planned as a "park" for participation, experience, and learning and includes a fun plaza, camping ground, restaurant, and lodge (see Figs. 3.23, 3.24, and 3.25). We hope in the long run to turn the park into a "park" for the enjoyment of nature as a beauty spot with 30,000 cherry trees.

Fig. 3.21 Fun Tube. (*Photo: Fujitsuka Mitsumasa.*)

Fig. 3.22 Cosmoland. (*Photo: Fujitsuka Mitsumasa.*)

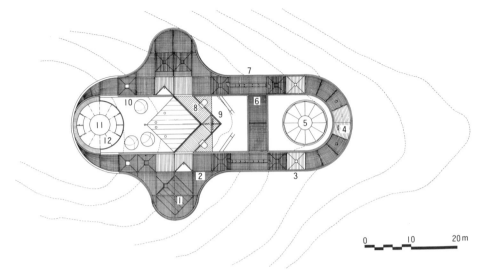

0   10   20 m

Fig. 3.23 Fun Plaza at Takebe no Mori Park. Plan: (1) Floating Floor, (2) Super Net, (3) Echo Tube, (4) Parabola, (5) Crater, (6) Slope Net, (7) Space Tube, (8) Wooden Deck, (9) Power-Generating Windmill, (10) Big Ball, (11) Big Tower, (12) Soft Floor.

Fig. 3.24 Takebe no Mori Park. A giant hammock at the summit of the hill. (*Photo: Fujitsuka Mitsumasa.*)

Bentencho Waterland

This 150 m by 50 m indoor leisure pool was designed as a "park" for the enjoyment of indoor-type "dizziness." With a teflon roof to brighten the place, this is the largest indoor amusement pool in Japan. It was built as part of the redevelopment project for Bentencho, which is an older area of Osaka.

Unlike traditional leisure pools, it was designed with the concept of a pool for children, families, and young people to have fun while playing in and with water. The pool consists of a three-dimensional circular play system and has a "Sky River" running through the middle, which is transparent throughout and passes through the air at a height of 5 m. It is an "experience-type" pool where one can have the strange feeling of floating through the air and may be defined as a "dizziness" experience device set in a circular play system. (See Figs. 3.26 to 3.30.)

Fig. 3.25 Takebe no Mori Park. Looking at the giant sheet from below. (*Photo: Fujitsuka Mitsumasa.*)

SPACE FOR CHILDREN

Most children in Japan today—85 percent of children aged 12, according to one survey—have their own rooms at home. When I was a child, very few of my friends had rooms of their own. Ordinary people's houses in Japan were traditionally not divided according to their functions into bedrooms, for example, and living rooms. The same room with *tatami* mat flooring could serve as a living room, guest room, dining room, and bedroom. The house I grew up in had a floor area of only 43 square meters and two rooms for seven people to live in, but I never felt that it was too small. People today are beginning to think that children having their own rooms has led to the loss of opportunities for conversation between them and their parents and may be a cause of the tendency for children to be introverted.

Fig. 3.26 Bentencho Water Land. The "Sky River" suspended in midair—width: 4 m. (*Photo: Fujitsuka Mitsumasa.*)

Fig. 3.27 Bentencho Water Land. (*Photo: Fujitsuka Mitsumasa.*)

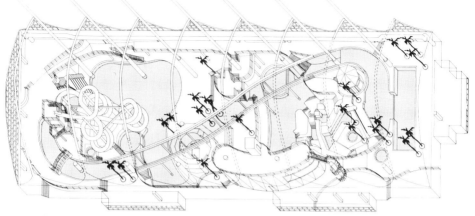

Fig. 3.28 Bentencho Water Land. Axonometric projection.

Fig. 3.29 Bentencho Water Land. Looking up at the Sky River through the transparent floor. (*Photo: Fujitsuka Mitsumasa.*)

Fig. 3.30 Bentencho Water Land. (*Photo: Fujitsuka Mitsumasa.*)

My belief is that we need to think about space for children according to their age.

The first stage is that of having a little spot of their own, for children up to the age of six or so. At this stage, children will demand to have their own little space in a corner of the living room, for example, in the form of a small table.

The second stage is that of having an area of their own. Children of primary school age will begin to have a desire to establish their own space in corners and alcoves. At this stage they are in the process of establishing spaces of their own.

In the third stage, children of junior high school age will demand to have their own "castles," and this may be thought of as the stage where they have established their own territories.

Kishakozo

This is a little desk I made for my own son (see Fig. 3.31). It may be thought of as a spatial device for children in the first stage mentioned above. There is a box for toys in the base and the seat is lifted 45 cm off the floor, so that the child will not always be looked down on by adults but will have his or her eyes at a height similar to theirs.

HOUSES FOR CHILDREN

I made a study in 1977 on what kind of play those who were adults now used to engage in at and near their homes in their childhood. My findings indicated that houses can be defined in terms of play as a (1) stage, (2) workshop, (3) exercise ground, and (4) hiding place.

When I talk of houses being stages for children's play activities, I mean that they must have spaces which can provide the background for children's imitation games, such as playing at being at school and playing

Fig. 3.31 Kishakozo. The boxcar below can be used to put toys in. (*Photo: Fujitsuka Mitsumasa.*)

with dolls, whether it be for small children or for children in the lower grades of primary school. Twenty to thirty years ago, *engawa*** and *tokonoma*† provided the space for such play in Japanese houses. Houses need to have structures which can provide the stage for these games.

The requirement of a house as a workshop is about whether the house can satisfy the needs of children who want to have somewhere they can make plastic models or carry out little scientific experiments. In my experience, the *engawa* was an ideal place for such activities.

The function of the house as an exercise ground seems to me to be its most important

---

*Wooden decks in front of living rooms in traditional Japanese houses. Usually on south-facing sides of houses.

†Symbolic spaces in corners of drawing rooms in traditional Japanese houses. Usually about 2 square meters in area and used to display pictures and vases.

function for children. The ideal conditions for a house are that it be a place where children can run and roll around freely, is safe, has a certain amount of free space, and, for the purpose of older children (up to primary school age), that there be enough room for ball games.

Hiding is an indispensable element of children's play, and it is important that the house should have places where children can hide. Chasing and hiding are fundamental elements of playing, be it hide-and-seek or playing at being monsters. *Oshiire,** sheds, large drawers, attics, and spaces below floors† and storerooms all enrich children's play.

House at Kataseyama

This is my house (see Figs. 3.32 to 3.35). Because of the lack of land in Japan, the average area per house is small at around 200 square meters. My house has an area of 680 square meters, but only 200 square meters of it is on level ground, the remaining 480 square meters being on a slope. There are bedrooms on the first floor, living room, kitchen, and a study on the second floor, and a 10-m pool and deck on the roof. The pool absorbs the radiant heat of the sun and keeps the living room below cool. There are woods in front of and behind the house.

Banana House

This is a small weekend house in a resort area 80 km or so from the center of Tokyo (see Figs. 3.36 to 3.38). The traditional large earth floor at the entrance to the house and the

---

*Storage space in traditional Japanese houses. Usually about 1.8 m long and 0.9 m wide.

†Floors are usually raised 0.5 to 0.9 m or more off the ground in traditional wooden houses in Japan to prevent rising dampness. Children sometimes use the space underneath the floor for their play.

Fig. 3.32 House at Kataseyama. The 10-m pool on the roof. (*Photo: Fujitsuka Mitsumasa.*)

Fig. 3.33 House at Kataseyama. The house has a pool on the roof.
(*Photo: Fujitsuka Mitsumasa.*)

Fig. 3.34 House at Kataseyama. Tent and pool. (*Photo: Fujitsuka Mitsumasa.*)

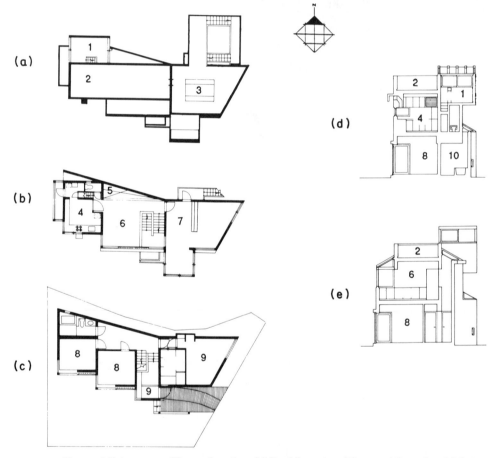

Fig. 3.35 House at Kataseyama. Plan and section. (*a*) Roof floor plan, (*b*) second floor plan, (*c*) first floor plan, (*d*) section, (*e*) section. (1) Sun room, (2) pool, (3) deck, (4) kitchen, (5) atrium, (6) living room, (7) study, (8) bedroom, (9) storage space, (10) bathroom.

Fig. 3.36 Entrance to the Banana House. (*Photo: Fujitsuka Mitsumasa.*)

Fig. 3.37 Banana House. The deck viewed from the inside. (*Photo: Fujitsuka Mitsumasa.*)

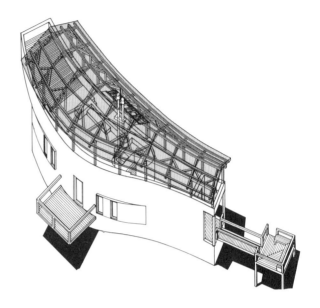

Fig. 3.38 Banana House. Axonometric projection.

Fig. 3.39 House at Yamato. Children can play on the deck. (*Photo: Shoukokusha Publishing Co., Ltd.*)

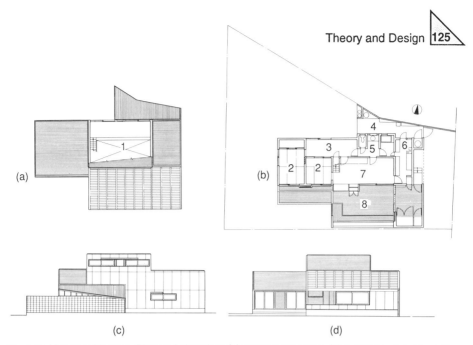

Fig. 3.40 House at Yamato. Plan and elevation: (*a*) second floor plan, (*b*) first floor plan, (*c*) north side elevation, (*d*) south side elevation.

deck on the second floor provide the nuclei of the house.

House at Yamato

The central space in the house at Yamato (Figs. 3.39 and 3.40) is the deck with a pergola. This is where the work in the house is done, where meals are taken, and where children play. The *engawa* and earth floors in traditional Japanese houses used to have important roles from the point of view of children's play. An *engawa* is a wooden deck located at the juxtaposition between the spaces inside and outside the house, and children's play used to be centered around here.

Onoba Housing Estate in Akita

Several proposals were made from the point of view of the children's play environment in the design of this municipal housing estate (Figs. 3.41 to 3.43).

Fig. 3.41 Onoba Housing Estate in Akita. A view of the courtyard from the stairway. The blocks are positioned in an irregular manner to give variation to the courtyards. (*Photo: Fujitsuka Mitsumasa.*)

Fig. 3.42 Onoba Housing Estate in Akita. A view of the courtyard from the road on the southeastern side of the estate. There is a playhouse for children at the center of the courtyard. (*Photo: Fujitsuka Mitsumasa.*)

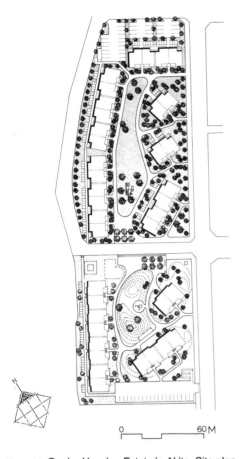

Fig. 3.43 Onoba Housing Estate in Akita. Site plan.

1. The blocks are positioned around a courtyard but the courtyard is not completely enclosed.

2. People can walk through the first floor of each block.

3. The sheds are built as separate buildings near the entrances to the blocks.

4. The courtyard has a playground for children centering around a grass hillock and a wooden playhouse.

Fig. 3.44 Sueyoshi Riverside Terrace. (*Photo: Fujitsuka Mitsumasa.*)

These conditions were based on the principles of the circular play system. Children must be able to pass through buildings, make shortcuts or detours, and have spaces where they can hide near their homes. Stairways too are important elements in children's play.

Sueyoshi Riverside Terrace

This housing estate is located in Naha, the southernmost major city in Japan (Figs. 3.44 and 3.45). Positive efforts were made to use the roads and adjoining areas as spaces for children's play, while preserving the traditional landscape in this housing estate,

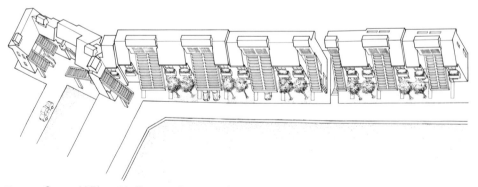

Fig. 3.45 Sueyoshi Riverside Terrace. Axonometric projection. The car park space provides a space for children.

which was designed mainly for people in their thirties and forties. Land prices are high in Japan, and in this housing estate too, the site area per household falls below 100 square meters.

Tomishiro Townhouse

This is a housing estate developed by a private enterprise in Tomishiro, a municipality adjoining Naha (see Figs. 3.46 and 3.47). The first floors are taken up by *pilotis* and courtyards, with dwelling units on second and third floors. The car parks and the courtyards provide spaces for children to play in.

ARCHITECTURE FOR CHILDREN

My view is that architecture and play structures are the same for children. The theory of circular play systems is valid also in the design of architecture for children. It was only in 1982 that I came to believe in the theory of circular play systems but some of my earlier architectural works, such as Nonaka Nursery School, Akagi House of Nature for Young People, and Ishikawa

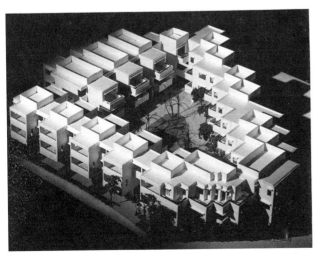

Fig. 3.46 Tomishiro Townhouse. (*Photo: Fujitsuka Mitsumasa.*)

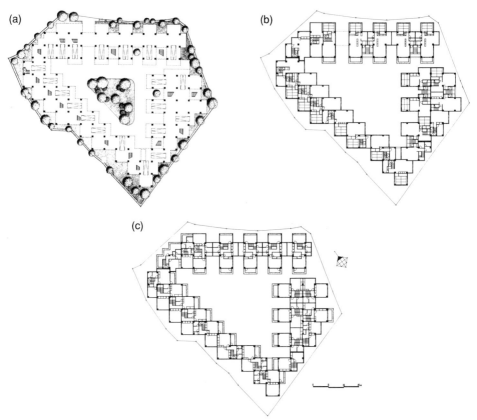

Fig. 3.47 Tomishiro Townhouse. Plan: (*a*) first floor plan, (*b*) second floor plan, (*c*) third floor plan.

House of Nature for Young People, also have circular play systems.

Here I discuss the three methods for creation of architecture for children.

"Earth Architecture"

I wanted to make buildings a place you can walk around and enjoy. For this reason, not only the stairways but all floor spaces were joined together by slopes. Slopes allow us to have that basic relationship with the ground of walking upon it. For children in particular, it makes possible the important activity of running around.

For children, there are no boundaries

Fig. 3.48 Viewpoint Plaza at Atagoyama Children's Land—a 30 m by 100 m plaza on a hill protruding into the city of Kofu. (*Photo: Shoukokusha Publishing Co., Ltd.*)

between buildings, parks, and roads. They do not consider it strange if what was a road a moment ago turns into a park and then into a building. I call such architectural structures "earth architecture."

Theater Architecture

I tried to turn the ground into an indoor space by giving the building a large roof. It is a theater with a large roof, consisting of steps and a stage. Steps have a special meaning for children. They provide gathering places, viewpoints, places to play, places for taking souvenir photographs, as well as being mini theaters in themselves. Steps provide

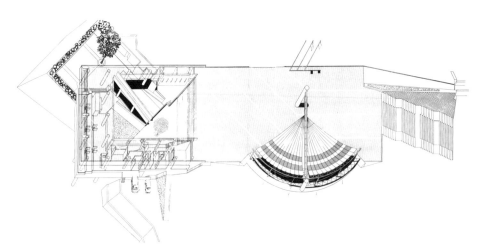
multipurpose settings par excellence for staging of dramas, and given that children's play activities are always a kind of drama, steps are important settings for children's play.

Circular Play Architecture

Circular play architecture is a circular play system realized in the form of buildings. Circular play architecture has the following five characteristics.

Circular Design. The most important factor in the circular play system is its circulatory function. In an architectural space this is provided mainly by corridors. The circle itself may be two- or three-dimensional. The Hamamatsu Science Museum has a flat circle, while a three-dimensional circle is provided by the raised corridor at the Nonaka Nursery School. What is important in either case is the composition of the corridors.

Expression of "Dizziness" in Architecture. Largely speaking, five types of dizziness experience can be incorporated into

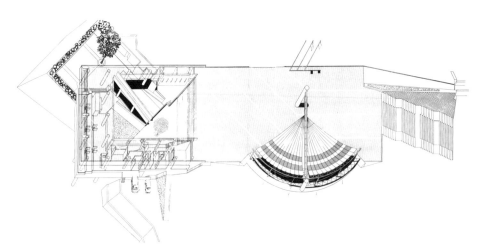

Fig. 3.49 Viewpoint Plaza at Atagoyama Children's Land. Axonometric projection.

Fig. 3.50 House of Nature for Young People at Atagoyama Children's Land. A perpendicular triangle protruding out of the hillside. (*Photo: Fujitsuka Mitsumasa.*)

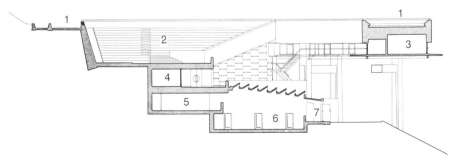

Fig. 3.51 House of Nature for Young People at Atagoyama Children's Land. Section. Bedrooms take up two sides of the triangle: (1) terrace road, (2) theater plaza, (3) bedrooms, (4) residents' lobby, (5) exhibit room, (6) main hall lobby, (7) main hall entrance.

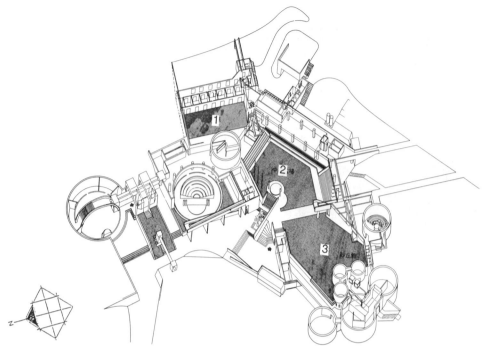

Fig. 3.52 Sand Dunes Children's Land. Axonometric projection: (1) courtyard, (2) central plaza, (3) Sand Dunes Museum.

Fig. 3.53 Sand Dunes Children's Land. (*Photo: Tomio Ohashi.*)

Fig. 3.54 Sand Dunes Children's Land. Interior of the Children's Theater. (*Photo: Tomio Ohashi.*)

Fig. 3.55 The entrance to the Iriki-cho Children's Center. (*Photo: Shoukokusha Publishing Co., Ltd.*)

Fig. 3.56 The outdoor hall at the Children's Center. (*Photo: Shoukokusha Publishing Co., Ltd.*)

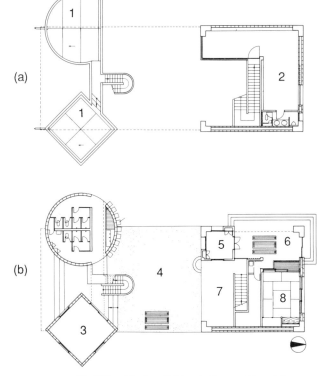

Fig. 3.57 Kushikino Marine Children's Center. Plan: (*a*) second floor plan, (*b*) first floor plan. (1) Roof, (2) library, (3) meeting room, (4) playing space, (5) office, (6) terrace, (7) stage, (8) Japanese-style room.

Fig. 3.58 Kushikino Marine Children's Center. The children's center and a Giant Stairway play structure. (*Photo: Fujitsuka Mitsumasa.*)

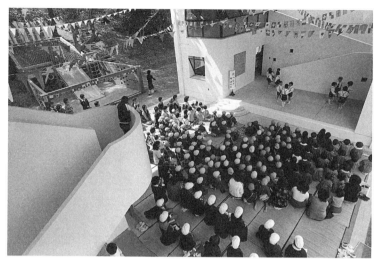

Fig. 3.59 Kushikino Marine Children's Center. An event put on by kindergarten children. (*Photo: Fujitsuka Mitsumasa.*)

architecture: (1) swinging, (2) being in a high place, (3) being on a slope, (4) being in a tunnel, and (5) being in a maze.

Expression of Variety in Space. Important elements of spatial variety in children's play include both visual variety such as variety of visual points, sizes and heights of spaces, feeling of freedom and brightness, as well

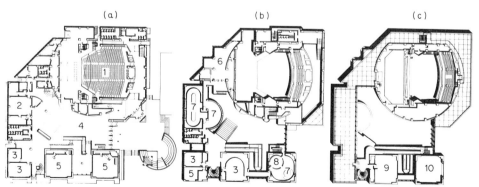

Fig. 3.60 Akita Prefectural Children's Center. Plan: (*a*) first floor plan, (*b*) second floor plan, (*c*) third floor plan. (1) Auditorium, (2) office, (3) laboratory, (4) Recreation hall, (5) craft room, (6) library, (7) exhibition room, (8) planetarium, (9) music room.

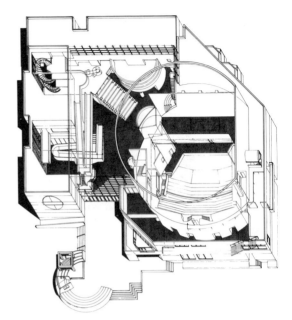

Fig. 3.61 Akita Prefectural Children's Center.
Axonometric projection.

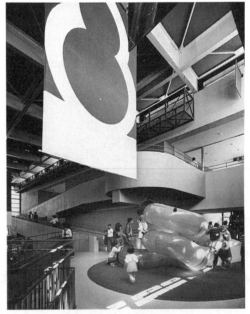

Fig. 3.62 Akita Prefectural Children's Center.
(*Photo: Fujitsuka Mitsumasa.*)

Fig. 3.63 Interior of the Akita Prefectural Children's Center. (*Photo: Fujitsuka Mitsumasa.*)

Fig. 3.64 Exterior of the Akita Prefectural Children's Center. (*Photo: Katsuaki Furudate.*)

Fig. 3.65 Exterior of the new block at Nonaka Nursery School. (*Photo: Fujitsuka Mitsumasa.*)

Fig. 3.66 Interior of the new block at Nonaka Nursery School.

平面図　floor plan

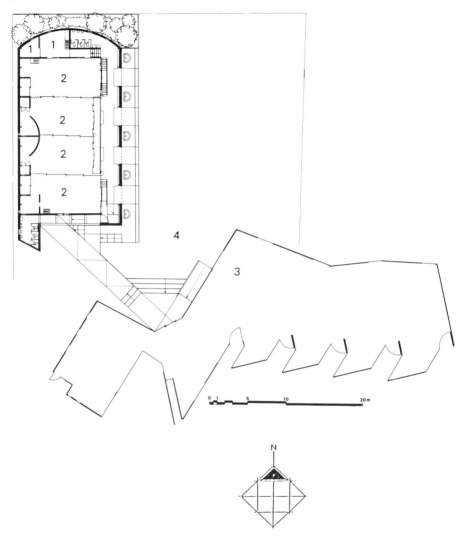

Fig. 3.67 New block at Nonaka Nursery School. Plan: (1) store, (2) nursery rooms, (3) old nursery building, (4) ground.

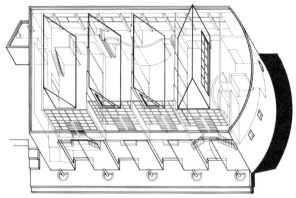

Fig. 3.68 New block at Nonaka Nursery School. Axonometric projection.

Fig. 3.69 North side of Nonaka Nursery School. (*Photo: The Japan Architect Shinkenchiku-sha Co., Ltd.*)

as variety in sound and light.

This variety is needed because variation arouses activity in children. Variety excites children's imagination.

Variation of Symbols. Symbols are required as points of variation in the flow of play both inside and outside buildings. Symbols of play are found concentrated in towerlike and stagelike structures.

Shortcuts Activating Space. Be it in buildings or outdoor spaces, variety of flow lines in the circle and the availability of a choice of paths are indispensable to children's play.

Since play is movement, it has a certain directivity and power. When the movement has become too concentrated—when, for example, several children are running together in one direction—the shortcut prevents the movement from turning into chaos and allows it to continue to flow smoothly. The shortcut route should ideally be different from the normal route; the use of a tunnel or a

Fig. 3.70 Nonaka Nursery School. (*Photo: The Japan Architect Shinkenchiku-sha Co., Ltd.*)

Fig. 3.71 Nonaka Nursery School. Sliding down the pole from the terrace. The sliding pole is a device for children's activity. (*Photo: The Japan Architect Shinkenchiku-sha Co., Ltd.*)

Fig. 3.72 Nonaka Nursery School. Looking down on the nursery room from the mezzanine terrace. (*Photo: The Japan Architect Shinkenchiku-sha Co., Ltd.*)

Fig. 3.73 Nonaka Nursery School.

suspension bridge for the shortcut will give a feeling of "dizziness" and make the shortcut feel like a shortcut. Following are examples of circular plan structures.

ViewPoint Plaza at Atagoyama Children's Land

This is a rectangular plaza 100 m in length and 30 m in width, with a restaurant at one end (see Figs. 3.48 and 3.49). There is a fine view over the city of Kofu from the plaza and the restaurant.

Fig. 3.74 Nonaka Nursery School. The corridor can be turned into a workshop. (*Photo: Yoshio Shiratori.*)

Fig. 3.75 Interior of the Nonaka Nursery School. (*Photo: Yoshio Shiratori.*)

Fig. 3.76 Nonaka Nursery School. (*Photo: Yoshio Shiratori.*)

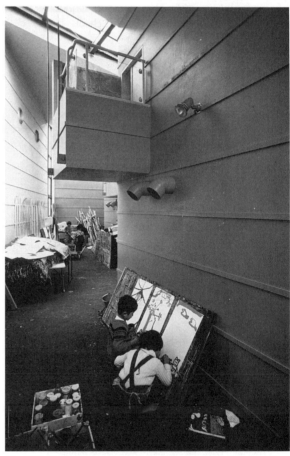

Fig. 3.77 Nonaka Nursery School. The promenade is a gallery for children. (Photo: Fujitsuka Mitsumasa.)

Fig. 3.78 Interior of the Nonaka Nursery School.

Fig. 3.79 Interior of the Nonaka Nursery School.

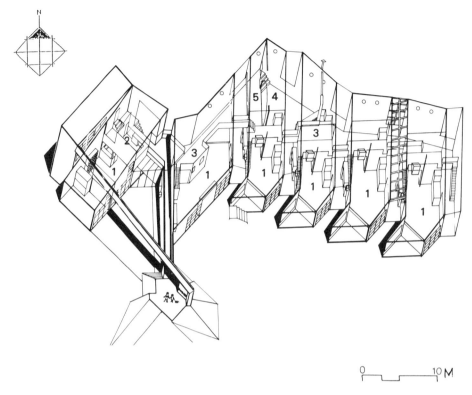

0 ⌐____⌐____⌐ 10 M

Fig. 3.80 Nonaka Nursery School. Axonometric projection: (1) nursery rooms, (2) office, (3) terrace, (4) promenade, (5) stage.

House of Nature for Young People at Atagoyama Children's Land

This house is located on the opposite side of an arc from the Viewpoint Plaza which is at the eastern end of the Children's Land (see Figs. 3.50 and 3.51). The house, with an area of 2500 square meters, can accommodate 200 children. Protruding from the slope, it has a stepped roof and was designed in the form of "earth architecture."

Children's Center and Sand Dunes Museum at Sand Dunes Children's Land

Two buildings, with a total floor area of 4700 square meters, form the central feature in the Children's Land (Figs. 3.52 to 3.54). The

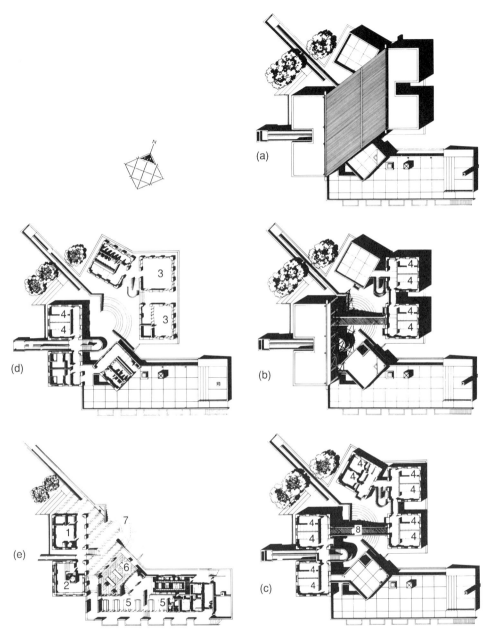

Fig. 3.81 Ishikawa House of Nature for Young People. Plans: (a) roof plan, (b) roof and third floor plan, (c) third and second floor plan, (d) second and first floor plan, (e) first floor plan. (1) Office, (2) library, (3) laboratories, (4) bedrooms, (5) dining room, (6) outdoor dining room, (7) spiral staircase, (8) bridge.

Fig. 3.82 Exterior of the Ishikawa House of Nature for Young People. (*Photo: Shoukokusha Publishing Co., Ltd.*)

Fig. 3.83 Central Hall at the Ishikawa House of Nature for Young People. (*Photo: Shoukokusha Publishing Co., Ltd.*)

Fig. 3.84 Ishikawa House of Nature for Young People. Central Hall with an overhead bridge. (*Photo: Shoukokusha Publishing Co., Ltd.*)

Fig. 3.85 Ishikawa House of Nature for Young People. (*Photo: Shoukokusha Publishing Co., Ltd.*)

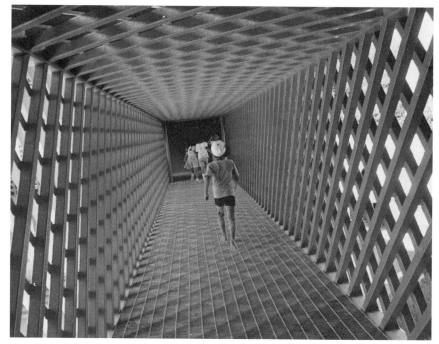

Fig. 3.86 Ishikawa House of Nature for Young People. The bridge connecting the two residential blocks. (*Photo: Fujitsuka Mitsumsa*

Fig. 3.87 Central Hall at the Akagi Outdoor School. (*Photo: Tomio Ohashi.*)

Fig. 3.88 Akagi Outdoor School. A view of the exterior at night. (*Photo: Tomio Ohashi.*)

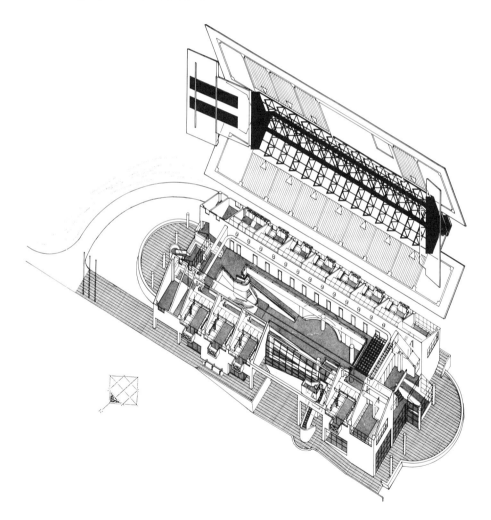

Fig. 3.89 Akagi Outdoor School. Axonometric projection.

(a)

(b)

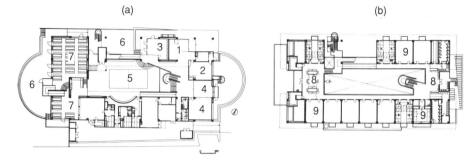

Fig. 3.90 Akagi Outdoor School. Plan: (*a*) first floor plan, (*b*) second floor plan. (1) Entrance, (2) office, (3) library, (4) laboratory, (5) hall, (6) terrace, (7) dining room, (8) conversation corner, (9) bedrooms.

Fig. 3.91 North side exterior of Yokohama Science Center. (*Photo: The Japan Architect Shinkenchiku-sha Co., Ltd.*)

Fig. 3.92 South side exterior of Yokohama Science Center.

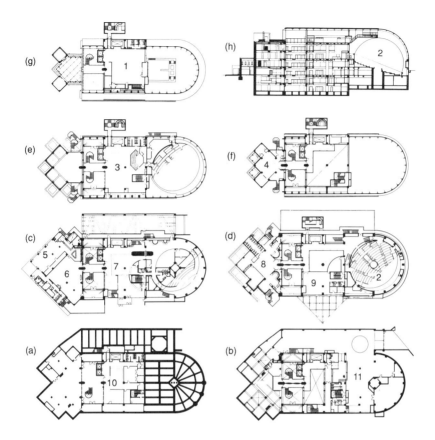

Fig. 3.93 Yokohama Science Center. Plans: (a) second basement plan, (b) first basement plan, (c) first floor plan, (d) second floor plan, (e) third floor plan, (f) fourth floor plan, (g) fifth floor plan, (h) section. (1) Space Captain, (2) Space Theater, (3) Space Gym, (4) Space City Yokohama, (5) coffee shop, (6) Space Gallery, (7) entrance hall, (8) Space Lab, (9) office, (10) Space Factory, (11) parking.

Fig. 3.94 Aerial view of Yokohama Science Center.

Fig. 3.95 Interior of Yokohama Science Center.

Fig. 3.96 Interior of Yokohama Science Center.

Fig. 3.97 Interior of Yokohama Science Center.

Sand Dunes Museum has a display of exhibits related to sand dunes. The roof is a spherical concrete dome constructed by concrete placement using an air membrane.

Irikicho Children's Center

This building, with a floor area of 182 square meters, was constructed on a small hill in a town in the northeastern part of Kagoshima Prefecture (see Figs. 3.55 and 3.56). There are two cylinders with the same length and diameter as a Boeing 737 jet held in midair, and these cylinders provide the space for children to play in. The whole forms a large gate, and the area around the bottom of the gate can be used as a stage, giving a theatrical spatial composition.

Kushikino Marine Children's Center

The playground underneath the huge roof takes up a large portion of the 300-square-meter floor area of the Kushikino Marine Children's Center (Figs. 3.57 to 3.59). This may be called an outdoor hall and is used for a variety of events. It functions as a resting place with a large shade during the bathing season in the summer and can be used for group play by children on rainy days.

Akita Prefectural Children's Center

A 400-seat hall and a children's science museum are found together at the Central Children's Center for Akita Prefecture (Figs. 3.60 to 3.64). A huge roof was provided to create a little town underneath for children in this northern city where snow hinders their outdoor play in winter.

New Block at Nonaka Nursery School

This building was designed to function not only as a nursery room but also as a theater and several devices have been installed to create stages for children's play. (See Figs.

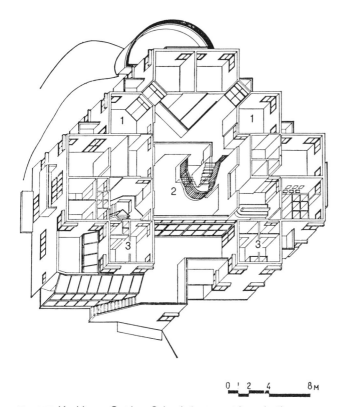

0 1 2 4 8 M

Fig. 3.98 Yoshiwara Outdoor School. Axonometric projection: (1) bedrooms, (2) recreation hall, (3) family rooms.

Fig. 3.99 North side of Yoshiwara Outdoor School.

Fig. 3.100 Yoshiwara Outdoor School.

Fig. 3.101 Yoshiwara Outdoor School.

3.65 to 3.68.) Opening and closing the large sliding doors and the large roof according to seasons, a number of stages can be provided for children to act on. Children will be filled with excitement and expectation that something new is about to start, as they watch the nursery where they spend their daily lives turning into something completely different.

Nonaka Nursery School

The rooms in this nursery (Figs. 3.69 to 3.80), while being independent facilities, are joined together by two circular flow lines. The large corridor on the north side is not straight but curved and has stages, steps, and balconies attached to it. The corridor with a low ceiling where only children can pass and which joins the mezzanine floors creates a three-dimensional circular play system. The sliding bars in the nursery rooms provide the shortcuts.

Ishikawa House of Nature for Young People

This is the central residential facility at an outdoor activity center for children in

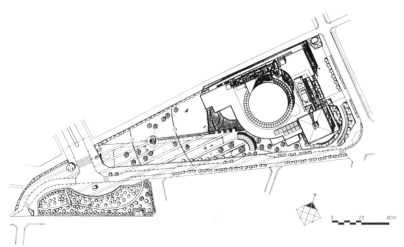

Fig. 3.102 Hamamatsu Science Museum Site plan.

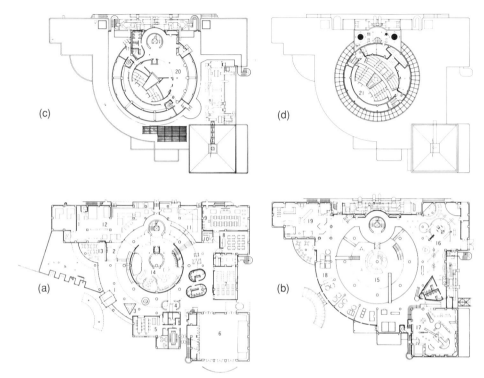

Fig. 3.103 Hamamatsu Science Museum. Plan: (a) first floor plan, (b) second floor plan, (c) third floor plan, (d) fourth floor plan. (1) Entrance hall, (2) information, (3) museum shop, (4) reading room, (5) office, (6) auditorium, (7) lecture room, (8) classroom, (9) workshop, (10) radio room, (11) electric room, (12) machinery room, (13) resting place, (14) exhibition room 1 "Nature," (15), exhibition room 2 "Cosmos," (16) exhibition room 3 "Electronics," (17) exhibition room 4 "Sound," (18) exhibition room 5 "Dynamics," (19) exhibition room 6 "Optics," (20) lobby, (21) planetarium.

Okinawa Prefecture, the southernmost prefecture in Japan made up of a chain of islands (see Figs. 3.81 through 3.86). Here the idea was not to create a hotel but a town for children. The large roof makes a shade in the yard. The complex as a whole has the form of a piece of circular play architecture as well as theatrical architecture.

Akagi Outdoor School

This building provides accommodation for outdoor activities for up to 200 children (see Figs. 3.87 to 3.90). There are symbolic totem poles and steps at either end of a large 13 m by 20 m space in the middle. With basketball

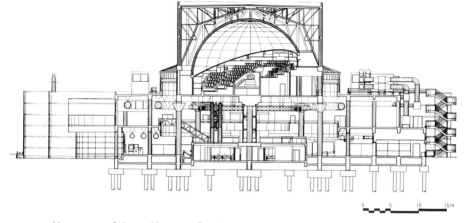

Fig. 3.104 Hamamatsu Science Museum. Section.

Fig. 3.105 Western side of the Hamamatsu Science Museum. (*Photo: Fujitsuka Mitsumasa.*)

Fig. 3.106 Hamamatsu Science Museum. Steps made of stones from the Tenryu River. (*Photo: Fujitsuka Mitsumasa.*)

goals and badminton nets in place it functions as an indoor sports hall on rainy days. All functional rooms are situated facing this space in the middle.

Yokohama Science Center

This science center for children uses the theme of the universe (see Figs. 3.91 to 3.97). What is meant by the universe here is not so much the universe in terms of space exploration and development as the universe as understood scientifically in terms of the relationship between human beings and their

Fig. 3.107 Hamamatsu Science Museum. Exhibition room 1 "Nature." (*Photo: Fujitsuka Mitsumasa.*)

Fig. 3.108 Hamamatsu Science Museum. Exhibition room 1 "Nature." (*Photo: Fujitsuka Mitsumasa.*)

Fig. 3.109 Hamamatsu Science Museum. Exhibition room 4 "Sound." (*Photo: Fujitsuka Mitsumasa.*)

Fig. 3.110 Hamamatsu Science Museum. Exhibition room 6 "Optics." (*Photo: Fujitsuka Mitsumasa.*)

Fig. 3.111 Interior of the Hamamatsu Science Museum. (*Photo: Fujitsuka Mitsumasa.*)

Fig. 3.112 Hamamatsu Science Museum. The planetarium surrounded by toplights. (*Photo: The Japan Architect Shinkenchiku-sha Co., Ltd.*)

environment. This is shown in a line going from human beings to Yokohama, Japan, Earth, the Solar System, and the Universe. It was inspired by the idea of "Spaceship Earth" proposed by Buckminster Fuller.

The composition of the subthemes, "Space Captain," "Space Gym," "Space Factory," "Space City" Yokohama, "Space Gallery," and "Space Theater" was intended to enable children who are not good at science at school to tackle the subject from fields which they like. The space theater in particular has a mechanism called "Omnimax," which combines the traditional planetarium with dome projection.

The building, consisting of two floors below ground and five above, forms a three-dimensional circular play system.

Yoshiwara Outdoor School

This is a short-term treatment facility for

Fig. 3.113 Hamamatsu Science Museum. Children can see the machinery room too. (*Photo: Fujitsuka Mitsumasa.*)

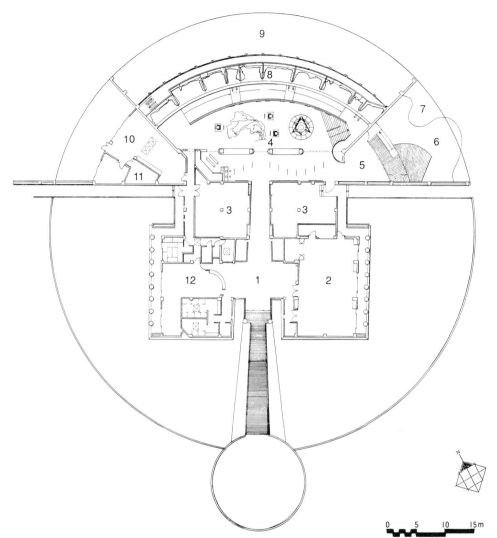

Fig. 3.114 Sagamigawa River Museum. Plan: (1) Entrance hall, (2) lecture hall, (3) machinery room, (4) exhibition room, (5) resting place, (6) touching pool, (7) aquatic plants, (8) streaming aquarium, (9) landscape gardening, (10) breeding room, (11) storage, (12) ticket booth.

emotionally disturbed children, where children spend periods of time ranging between a month and a year (Figs. 3.98 to 3.101). The facilities were arranged so as to enable children with different problems—most of whom have problems at home or in

(a)

(b)

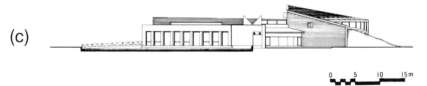

(c)

0 5 10 15 m

Fig. 3.115 Sagamigawa River Museum. Section: (a) south elevation, (b) north elevation, (c) east elevation.

Fig. 3.116 Aerial view of the Sagamigawa River Museum. (*Photo: Fujitsuka Mitsumasa.*)

Fig. 3.117 Entrance of the Sagamigawa River Museum. (*Photo: Fujitsuka Mitsumasa.*)

Fig. 3.118 Sagamigawa River Museum. Water tank.

Fig. 3.119 Sagamigawa River Museum. An *objet d' art* on the theme of water. (*Photo: Fujitsuka Mitsumasa.*)

their relationships with their parents—and of different age groups to build up close communities.

The large multipurpose play hall in the middle is surrounded by children's bedrooms. The stairs are designed as stages and can be used as settings for holiday and birthday parties. Complementing the large hall in the middle, the circular corridor, stagelike stairs, library corner, and doorways leading directly outside together form a porous circular play system.

Hamamatsu Science Museum

I made an attempt to apply the concept of circular play systems in as complete a form as possible at this science museum with a total floor area of 7000 square meters (see Figs. 3.102 to 3.113).

Around the circular stylobate below the planetarium in the middle are a number of voids with toplights and display rooms. The central stylobate and the surrounding display rooms are connected by play-structure-like flow lines. The museum as a whole comprises a series of concentric circles. The first floor accommodates the machinery room, workshop, lecture hall, laboratory, administration room, hall, toilets, shops, and resting place, for all of which entrance is free. For the exhibit rooms, one goes 1.2 m down from the first floor and goes below the central stylobate, where the low ceilings create an enclosed space. One has to pay to enter the display space from here on.

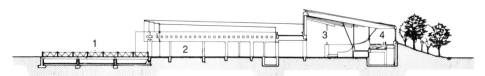

Fig. 3.120 Sagamigawa River Museum. Section. The water tank creates a visual flow continuous with the greenery outside. (1) Bridge, (2) entrance hall, (3) exhibition room, (4) water tank.

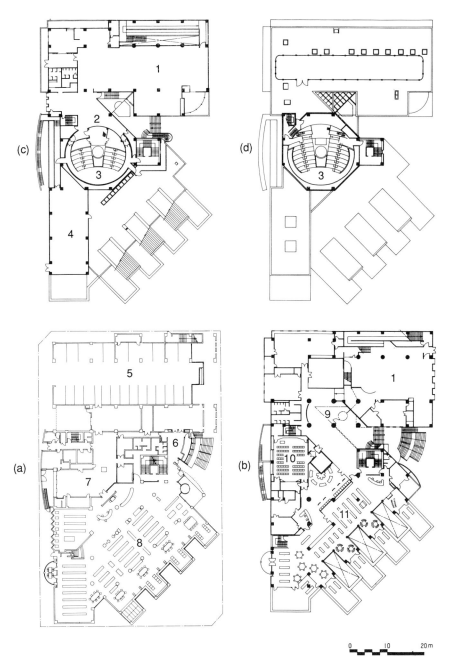

Fig. 3.121 Isehara Library and Science Museum. Plan: (*a*) first floor plan, (*b*) second floor plan, (*c*) third floor plan, (*d*) fourth floor plan. (1) Exhibition room, (2) planetarium lobby, (3) planetarium, (4) machinery room, (5) parking, (6) library lobby, (7) library office, (8) library, (9) information corner, (10) audiovisual room, (11) children's library.

Fig. 3.122 Isehara Library and Science Museum. (*Photo: The Japan Architect Shinkenchiku-sha Co., Ltd.*)

Fig. 3.123 Exterior of Isehara Library and Science Museum. (*Photo: The Japan Architect Shinkenchiku-sha Co., Ltd.*)

The area underneath the stylobate is the nature display space, where one can view the exhibits to do with nature in and around Hamamatsu from various angles. Walking up the stairs made of stones from the Tenryu River, which flows to the east of Hamamatsu, we come out on top of the stylobate, where we find the space corner. From here we can enter the surrounding exhibit rooms by crossing bridges. There is a circular flow line through the exhibit rooms, which are divided into four corners for light, sound, power, and electronics. To arrive at the planetarium, we go up another floor either via the circular stairway or by an elevator. As far as possible, the exhibits are placed away from the walls so that people can pass behind them. In other words, the exhibits are positioned like islands among the circular flow lines to create a "porous" space. As a result, there is no specific route one has to follow around the exhibit rooms. Children can wander around and "experience" the exhibits at will and in doing so will constantly be discovering new spaces and devices. I designed the space inside the building using the same concept as that for circular play systems.

In accordance with the concept that the

Fig. 3.124 Interior of Isehara Library and Science Museum.

Fig. 3.125 Isehara Library and Science Museum. Audiovisual room. (*Photo: The Japan Architect Shinkenchiku-sha Co., Ltd.*)

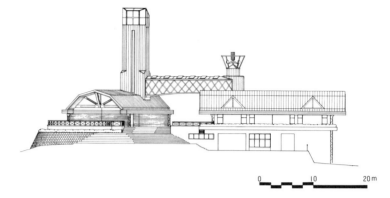

Fig. 3.126 Center House at Toriidaira Yamabiko Park. Elevation.

building itself is a scientific exhibit, the machinery room was positioned right by the entrance to the exhibit rooms and architectural features including not only the ducts but also the mechanisms at the tops of elevators and automatic doors, concrete columns, and the ceiling for the laboratory were placed in such a way that children could observe how they work. Even the automatic vendors are given transparent sides so as to make the mechanism inside visible. In order to clarify the functions of various features, architectural parts were left uncolored, while mechanical and functional parts were given specific colors.

The outside of the planetarium, which comprises the skyline of the building, was given a look appropriate for a science museum by covering the concrete exterior walls and roof with aluminum panels. Picture elements are provided by creating rectangular protrusions 1 cm in width, 4 cm in length, and 5 mm in thickness on the cylindrical aluminum panels. Sunlight reflected by the picture elements produce pictures of various figures including the face of Einstein. The pictures cannot be seen on cloudy and rainy days. The figures which appear on sunny days vary according to angles, time of day,

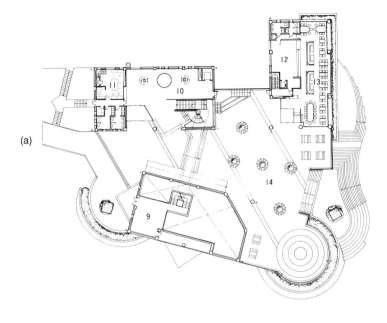

(a)

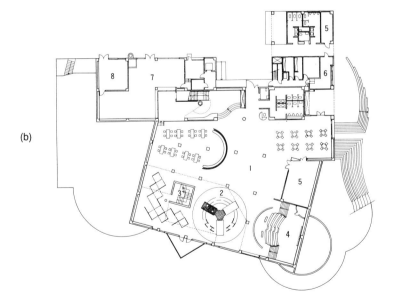

(b)

Fig. 3.127 Center House at Toriidaira Yamabiko Park. Plan: (*a*) second floor plan, (*b*) first floor plan. (1) Main hall, (2) play structure, (3) observation tower, (4) audiovisual corner, (5) storage, (6) shop, (7) machinery room, (8) electricity room, (9) rest area, (10) information, (11) office, (12) kitchen, (13) restaurant, (14) fine view terrace.

Fig. 3.128 Center House at Toriidaira Yamabiko Park. (*Photo: Fujitsuka Mitsumasa.*)

and seasons, the figures sometimes appearing as positives and sometimes as negatives.

The raster tiles are made concave to produce a maximum variation in color as they reflect the sunlight. They contain devices for wind and solar power generation, and an attempt was made to harmonize the exterior of the building and the exhibits inside.

Sagamigawa River Museum

This facility, with a site area of 1 ha and a floor area of 1500 square meters, is a

Fig. 3.129 Interior of the Center House at Toriidaira Yamabiko Park. (*Photo: Fujitsuka Mitsumasa.*)

freshwater aquarium combined with a museum of rivers (see Figs. 3.114 to 3.120). A tank is on display in which the 109-km Sagami River is represented over a length of 40 m. The tank is divided into sections for the upper, middle, and lower reaches of the river, with cascades in between, and the model can be viewed from the slope climbing up beside it, allowing children to observe the river at various heights. The building as a whole comprises a circular play system.

Fig. 3.130 Center House at the Central Children's Land. Plan: (*a*) second floor plan, (*b*) first floor plan. (1) Dining hall, (2) terrace, (3) office, (4) kitchen, (5) shop, (6) bathroom, (7) toilet, (8) storage, (9) barbecue stove, (10) barbecue terrace, (11) linen closet, (12) bedrooms.

Isehara Library and Science Museum

This complex in Isehara, an outer suburb of Tokyo with a population of 80,000, consists of the three facilities for use by the citizens and children of the area (see Figs. 3.121 to 3.125), the central municipal library, children's science museum, and information center. The library comprises a relatively static space and the children's science museum a more active one. With an information center in addition to these two facilities with contrasting functions, the complex as a whole was designed as a base for the provision of information. Each of the two facilities on the outside has its own circular flow lines, and the information center was positioned at the junction between the two.

Center House at Toriidaira Yamabiko Park

This is the central facility at Toriidaira Yamabiko Park, which functions as an information center, restaurant, audiovisual corner, and play and exhibition corner (Figs. 3.126 to 3.129). The left and right wings are connected at the first floor level, while the viewing towers in the two wings are joined by a glass bridge, making it possible to enjoy a variety of views from inside the building.

Center House at the Central Children's Land

The Center House, situated on high ground by an artificial lake, provides accommodation for children and families (see Figs. 3.130 to 3.132). It is a wooden, two-story building with room for about 60 people. The twelve guest rooms are located on the second story with better ventilation and views, while the office, dining room, showers, and toilets are found below on the first floor. The two floors

Fig. 3.131 Center House at the Central Children's Land. (*Photo: Fujitsuka Mitsumasa.*)

Fig. 3.132 Center House at the Central Children's Land. Outdoor Activities Center. A house for 60 children. (*Photo: Fujitsuka Mitsumasa.*)

are connected with two sets of stairs, with the corridors being on the opposite sides of the building on each floor, making for a change of views and creating a circular play system.

POSTSCRIPT

This book deals with the concepts born of my studies on children's play environments over a period of 23 years from 1968 to 1990, and examples of design based on them. Each piece of work has its merits and failings, but each brings back fond memories to me. I have always wanted to create cities and spaces where children can play to their hearts' content. I am very happy to be able to compile the results of my work into a book such as this. All the examples illustrated in this book are the fruits of my work in cooperation with the staff of the Environment Design Institute, to whom much gratitude is due. I am also grateful to Mari Ogi of the Environment Design Institute and Joel Stein of McGraw-Hill for their generous advice and help.

I hope this little book will be of use in the creation and formation of satisfactory play environments for children who are to be the builders of the twenty-first century.

INDEX

ABOUT THE AUTHOR

Mitsuru Senda is president of the Environmental Design Institute in Tokyo, Japan and is a professor of the Nagoya Institute of Technology in the Department of Architecture and Urban Design in Aichi-ken, Japan. He has lectured extensively, has won several professional design awards, and has specialized for over 20 years in designing play apparatus and play environments for children.